PRAYING
FOR OTHERS

D0099388

PRAYING FOR OTHERS

Powerful Practices for
Healing, Peace, and New Beginnings

Birrell Walsh

A Crossroad 8th Avenue Book
The Crossroad Publishing Company
New York

The Crossroad Publishing Company
481 Eighth Avenue, New York, NY 10001

Copyright © 2003 by Birrell Walsh

All rights reserved. No part of this book may be reproduced, stored in a retrieval system, or transmitted, in any form or by any means, electronic, mechanical, photocopying, recording, or otherwise, without the written permission of The Crossroad Publishing Company.

This book is set in 11/14 Trump Mediaeval. The display fonts are University, Optima, and Gill Sans.

Printed in the United States of America

Library of Congress Cataloging-in-Publication Data
Walsh, Birrell.
    Praying for others / Birrell Walsh.
      p. cm.
    Includes bibliographical references.
    ISBN 0-8245-1949-3 (alk. paper)
    1. Intercessory prayer – Comparative studies. 2. Spiritual healing.
  I. Title.
    BL560.W35 2003
    291.4′3 – dc21

                                      2003006760

1 2 3 4 5 6 7 8 9 10   10 09 08 07 06 05 04 03

Wisdom,
Love,
Power

Show us the way
to kind action.

CONTENTS

CALLED TO BLESSING

*Traveling up through red-rock country of western Utah,
I asked what to do when I grew up. A voice in my mind
said, "Blessing."*
Thank you, Voice: Here's your book.

Vocations are funny things. They come to us without any
explanation. I'd always wondered what mine might be, and
I had asked myself that question innumerable times. As my
wife Nancy and I traveled across the Nevada desert and up
into Utah in April 1988, I had no idea that this time there
would be a reply. I was forty-four, and there never had been
an answer before.

This time there was, and this time it stuck. So for the past
fourteen years I've had the good fortune to have a purpose,
and to follow it through ten years of part-time study at the
very tolerant California Institute of Integral Studies in San
Francisco, through a 377-page dissertation about how eight
North Americans of various traditions pray for others,[1] and
through lots of questions. A television technician by profes-
sion and a cook by avocation, I am very interested in *how*
things are done. My temperament and the voice's advice
have driven my quest to find out how people pray for and
bless others.

This is the book I wish I could have found then. It talks
about different ways that one can pray for others.

There are three forms of prayer that I believe are known to everyone.

Gathering in congregational prayer

Speaking directly to the Holy, and

Repetitive prayer, like rosaries and mantras.

I have not dwelt on these three in this book, because I believe others teach them very well.

This book is about the other choices you have. There is information about feeling people at a distance, and about energy healing. You will hear about blessing by singing and "retrieving souls," about inviting others to help, about finding essential patterns, about unifying with God, and about offering suffering, energy, delight, and space. There is a section on finding guidance. It is a potluck on purpose, because it is at potlucks that you learn new recipes to try in your own home.

I think it is good to remain within your own tradition while looking at how others pray and bless. Most traditions have favorite ways to pray that they bring out and use again and again, while in forgotten records they have a treasure trove of ways they once used and can use again. If you find yourself attracted to a practice that seems to come from another tradition, please examine the history of your own faith. You are likely to find that there were once people in your own history who prayed in very much this way. This is a book about those other varieties of blessing, to add to what you already have.

The practice of praying for others teaches appreciation. You find yourself saying "Thank you!" a lot. You may not even know to Whom you are saying it, but the words will come frequently.

I am grateful to Nancy Grant, my wife, who encouraged me at each step and read every word with a sharp eye.

I was raised Roman Catholic, and I am grateful to the nuns and priests who lived long celibate lives serving their parishioners and students.

In college I spent time with Protestant youth groups and with Quakers who were deeply involved with very concrete service. Thanks to them for the witness they still bear.

In midlife I encountered the work of Lawrence LeShan. His groundbreaking research on healing[2] let me begin praying again, without leaving agnosticism.

I am grateful to the New Thought tradition. They helped to bring the idea of "practical prayer" into our minds by praying for healing, prosperity, and relationship for any who came to their practitioners' offices.

Julie Henderson's name comes up often in these pages. She is an American Buddhist and my teacher; she continues to be an amazingly generous guide.

Her students take part in a Buddhist online prayer list, of which I have had the privilege of being a postmaster. They have taught me the most about bringing every issue to the community to ask for prayer.

Deborah Klingbeil has been a friend for years, and she has shared much of her family's experience in prayer research with me.

Dozens of people shared their own stories. Many of them said I could use their names; a few preferred anonymity or even disguise. All were generous with their time and very personal experience.

Barbara Neighbors Deal of Literary Associates in Ojai, California, is the supportive, hardworking agent every author hopes for. Roy M. Carlisle of The Crossroad Publishing Company looked at an earlier draft and gently said,

"You know, I have a suggestion or two." They were good suggestions.

KQED, the public television station in San Francisco, has been a kindly employer for thirty-six years. Thanks to all of you who pledged; you made this book possible.

My mother, Alta Walsh, gave me my love for words.

The voice of the raven kept me company as I typed for hours. A powerful thing, that voice.

When you pray, you begin to realize that we do not pray alone. Above all, thanks to all the Invisible Friends. It turns out they are not just for children.

As you practice, I hope you will pray for me and for those I love. At this moment I pray for you and yours. Let us join, eventually, to bless all beings.

A WORD ABOUT BLESSING

Blessing is a practice of working subjectively for the subjective and objective benefit of others. All forms of blessing have in common the experience of invisible help, the discovery that your own subjective process can help people.

There are many ways to help people objectively, and those who do so are often heroes: the aid worker, the volunteer at a shelter, the nurse and the doctor, the social worker driving through the night to get a child home, the office worker who stops to give a dollar to the homeless, the adult child caring for a disabled parent, and the young parent caring for a helpless child.

Prayer for others is based on the experience that there is an additional kind of help, one that reaches from our inner world, picks up invisible assistance on the way, and arrives to comfort, help, and heal others.

Whether we've always experienced this inner world or find it in midlife, those of us who find it real naturally also want to use it to assist others. That is the second thing that all these forms of prayer have in common: the desire to be helpful. Helpfulness is a good attitude to have, I think, especially if tempered with respect; and it leads us to search inner experience to find ways to help others with inner hands.

Blessing is also *not* many things.

Blessing is not a replacement for objective action, for giving to the poor, helping those who need help, and being kind to the difficult. While some practitioners in this book would disagree, I think that blessing is not a replacement for standard medical care. Prayer works *with* these things and does not replace them.

Blessing is not the preserve of the saintly. You need not be virtuous to pray for others. Attending to the needs of others is, in itself, a good deed. But virtue is not a prerequisite.

Blessing is not something you have to be good at before you start, a talent from birth. People can *learn* to pray for others.

It is not something you have to be a believer to do. True, if you spend all your prayer-time saying "This will never work," you might get what you expect. But if you can get to even a tentative neutrality you may be surprised at how often your kind wishes for others come true.

 Matching Your Temperament

When I was in graduate school I noticed that the older a religious tradition was, the more forms of prayer it accepted. It might start out with one or two, but over time others would come in and be made welcome. When I first started to learn about different sorts of prayer and blessing, it seemed that there should be some unity to them, some overall pattern that they fit into. But it was never so. They always seemed to come from different worlds. It wasn't just that they came from different traditions, though of course they do. It was that they felt different. There was no qualitative unity to them. They were as different as tacos and tabouli.

There are (for instance) many names for the prayer that intercedes for other people: intercessory prayer, treatment, blessing, thinking good thoughts, giving energy, and even "humming." There are practices for the social person to do with a group, and some for the solitary to do alone. There are varieties for the voluble and the silent, for the person who likes to touch and the person who wants privacy. There are blessings based on vision, on feeling, on language; blessings for the believer and for the agnostic.

It finally dawned on me that the variety was not for the sake of the Holy, but for us. There are different kinds of prayer so that different kinds of people can take part. My experience in the kitchen teaches me that there is no end of ways to cook, many of them good, and each with its own story. Different people like different recipes, in prayer as in food, and that is why this book exists.

You don't have to like them all or even to try them all, any more than there is a need to cook everything in *Joy of Cooking.* May you find a blessing here that matches your temperament!

YOU DON'T HAVE TO BE ALONE

My friend "Pearl" loved Honey. Honey was a dog who had been found by the road, already growing old. Pearl had brought her home, cared for her, taken her traveling from continent to continent. Every medicine or treatment that might make Honey comfortable, Pearl bought. She was not a fanatic, but she did love her dog; and now Honey was dying. Then she called in tears and said her dog was gone.

I wondered what I could offer my friend at that moment. Sitting in my living room in the sad dark early evening, I reached out to be aware of Pearl and of Honey who had just died. I did nothing to try to change my friend, yet there was a feeling that she was less frantic and less lonely. She would mourn her friend, of course, but she would not have to mourn alone.

Then it was done. I could feel her tiredness, her ache, but also acceptance and gratitude for the support she had experienced. There would be other moments of company-keeping, but now it was time for me to go to bed, to sleep a little before the outward day begins. In the morning we might talk on the telephone, and perhaps visit.

Perhaps the simplest form of blessing is to keep company with another person. We sit by a bedside, or "visit orphans and widows in their distress,"[3] or simply spend time with those who are lonely. The logic of blessing someone at a distance suggests that we can do something in addition to that, by visiting in spirit people whom we cannot reach in person. My teacher (that would be Julie Henderson, an American Buddhist) has repeatedly asked her students to "keep company" with people who are miles or continents away. Haltingly, gradually, we have learned to do so.

Recall the feeling of being close to someone. Enter that feeling, and be close to that person even at great distances.

Can our minds and hearts and souls be with someone who is far away from us? Or is that forever a sweet, empty metaphor? I think it is possible.

It is more than just reaching across space. I think that there's a kind of loneliness that comes from being in bodies: we are identified with the inside of our experience. We wonder why others cannot perceive that interior, and why we cannot experience the inside of theirs. To bridge that separation, to perceive a part of another person's inner reality, is to breech that solitude. For those that welcome it — and not all people *do* welcome it — it is a genuine blessing.

In this chapter I will share some methods for initiating such contact, for accepting the subtle messages involved, for recognizing such communion when it is offered, for connecting while maintaining our own boundaries, and for ending the link when we've had enough. There are stories of making contact, but the point is to try out some of the methods in the stories. Any one of them might be the *very* method of blessing to which you are called.

Keeping company is not a matter of intelligence gathering, of spying on someone else. It is not even about collecting information so we can pray more effectively. It is simply being with the other person, the kind of friendly huddling together we all need as social beings. Perception and information are not always shared, and they serve only as validations of the contact.

 Caring for Strangers

I'll always be grateful for some things I learned in the *est* training in the early 1970s. This seminar program was created by Werner Erhard, from elements of other older teachings. One part of the graduation from the *est* seminar came (apparently) from the Silva Mind Control course.

We were all exhausted from a long weekend, in that altered state that lots of up-and-down seminar emotion can create, when hundreds of volunteers arrived. Each had graduated from *est* already, and there was one of them for each of us.

The volunteers sat with us and invited us to go to our "workshop," an imaginary space we had created by visualizing it throughout the training. When we "got there" in our imaginations, the volunteer asked us to bring a specific person onto the workshop's stage, a person who was known to the volunteer but not to us. When they arrived on the stage, we were to walk over to them, lift their head off their shoulders, and put it on over our own head.

I followed these instructions, and suddenly, surprisingly, found myself in the midst of someone else's personality. It was a woman, and I knew that she/I had red hair. I could feel her personality, more outgoing than mine and more aware of the temperature around her. I began to describe my experience to the volunteer, saying what it felt like to be this person.

When I opened my eyes, I found the volunteer open-mouthed in front of me. Apparently the description I had given of her friend on the East Coast was exactly accurate.

Like most people, I was a well-trained skeptic. I was certain that the volunteers had been told to go along with whatever we said, and that the whole thing was a fraud. Or, I should say, I was intellectually certain that it must be a fake. But the whole experience certainly *felt* real.

Some months later, I signed up to be a volunteer at a graduation. We went in for an evening's training. When the instructor spoke of the putting-on-the-head exercise we would be facilitating for the new graduates, he told us to choose someone we knew, and to give only their name and city of residence to the person graduating. We were not told to fake anything; in fact, we were not to telegraph any information at all.

These instructions convinced me that my own experience had been real — somehow I had "put on the head" of a person three thousand miles away from the San Francisco hotel room in which the training was being held. I had kept company with a complete stranger, and gotten to know how she felt.

And so can you. Like all the techniques described in this book, this story is intended as an exemplar. Because another person has gone there, you know that it is *possible* that you can too. If it works convincingly for you, you have a new way of blessing. If not, it means only that you may be called to a different part of the practice of blessing.

We always wonder if we are "just imagining" our contact with another person. Our culture supports that doubt, and if you're psychologically trained you may believe you are projecting your own feelings on the other person. But I have found that one of the most reliable marks of genuine contact is a sense of alienness.

If you visit a foreign country, there will be ways in which it is not like your own. Aromas will be different. The rhythms of life and the sounds in the street will be exotic, and the feeling of utensils and the taste of the food at mealtimes will not be like those in your own land.

In the same way there is a slight strangeness to someone else's experience. When you experience what another person does, you will feel other than you usually feel. The world may be brighter or dimmer, louder or quieter. Feelings may be stronger or more muted. The experience is genuinely, if perhaps subtly, *different* from your own. And that difference is a mark of real perception of someone else's world.

In perceiving that alienness, you're joining the other person in their own world. You are a visitor who will leave at some time in the future, but you have really come to know the other person. You are sure of it, and at some level they know it. You give, and receive, the blessing of reaching through the solitude we inherit as flesh-wearing beings.

 ## Unexpected Perceptions

As a volunteer at the graduation of others from *est,* I learned a lot about how people can block out the experience of contact — because many do. We don't do it out of resistance or unwillingness so much as out of habit, dismissing things if they come to us in a way other than what we're used to.

I gave the name of a roommate to one person who was graduating. The graduate's posture changed. He slumped and shifted his body. His face softened. In a moment he was doing an extremely good imitation of my roommate, a person he had never seen. And then he said, "I'm not getting anything."

From this session and others like it I learned that people have expectations about how they will get information. This graduate apparently expected to see or hear something, but instead the experience was coming to him as a body posture.

He was simply not noticing it, because it was not what he expected. When I told him that the body-posture he had assumed was exactly that of my roommate, he suddenly noticed, "Oh, yes. My posture *is* different than usual."

We each have different styles of perceiving the physical universe, and it is just as true when we venture into the universe of non-physical contact. Jacob dreamed visions and voices at Bethel,[4] and wrestled with God while wide-awake at Penuel.[5] Ezekiel saw clear visions, heard sounds and voices, and was lifted up by the Spirit.[6] Paul the Apostle heard a voice and saw only a blinding light.[7] What would have become of him if he had said, "No, messages are supposed to have clear pictures, as Ezekiel had! Just a voice and bright light are not enough."

If our experiences and our expectations coincide, we find it easy to believe our own subtle experiences. If we think we should be seeing something, and we do, then we can believe we are getting information. But if the experience and the expectation are different, we say to ourselves, "I'm not *really* getting any contact."

When the new graduate turned his attention to my roommate, his body picked up and modeled the posture of someone he had never seen. It's very difficult to assume a posture without feeling the attitude that goes with it, so his body was telling him about the attitude of another person. As he noticed that, he began to realize he had really touched another human so closely that he could even take on his posture and feelings.

When you open to keeping company, other senses may open. While doing interviews for this book I spoke with a Muslim *imam.* He spoke of spiritual aromas, something I had never experienced.

One day months later my friend "Ellen" was lamenting her difficulty in meeting attractive men. She is a striking woman, so she gets lots of attention for her beauty and her competence. But it was clear to me that Ellen was hiding the attractiveness of her soul because she is a very private person, yet it was her soul she wanted perceived and loved and desired.

Suddenly I could smell the odor of incense, intense and unmistakable, and with it came the words "incense tree." So I said to Ellen, "This may seem odd but..." and told her about the fragrance and the words. She smelled it too — "Almost like patchouli," she said.

To her this was a message that she could choose to be like the incense trees of Arabia, drawing men without advertising herself, by the "aroma" of her secret selfhood. For me, it was the first time I caught a whiff of another person's nature. And for both of us it was a moment of blessing, because the incense smell had been the way we kept a moment's company.

Things can suddenly draw your attention in new ways, *if you will accept them*. Take what you get. If you ask what is going on with someone in the distance, and a strange sense of gurgling in your intestine comes up — accept it as a thread leading to the answer.

I remember walking, when I was a teenager, by the ocean with a sense that there was another world nearby. It felt as if the world I could see was in front of a curtain, and behind it was another whole world that was just as real. This is just the often-cited experience William James expressed in his *Varieties of Religious Experience:* "Our normal waking consciousness, rational consciousness as we call it, is but one special type of consciousness, whilst all about it, parted from it by the filmiest of screens, there lie potential forms of consciousness entirely different."[8]

The other world through which we keep company is like the back of a tapestry. The physical world is like the tapestry's face. Threads that disappear from the physical world travel in the other world and then reappear in this one.

In this world we are separated by space and time, but in the second world, with its hidden threads, we are connected. Those reappearing threads are the tiny thoughts and feelings that arise with no explanation, the ones that make no sense, the ones that are easy to dismiss.

That small nagging distraction that just *can't* be important may be the message.

When Elijah was called to Mount Horeb, he was shown a great wind, then a great earthquake, then a great fire. But the Lord was not in those. It was with the "still small voice" that he was to converse and keep company, and when he heard that small voice he went out of his cave.[9] And so it is often in very tiny voices that we find the threads of connection with the Holy and with each other.

These tiny half-perceived awarenesses are what psychologist and teacher Arnold Mindell calls "flirtations." They are very subtle invitations from a larger reality inviting you to communicate with it. They can seem to come from another person, in which case you are invited to communicate with that person. But they can also come from animals, from plants, from places, or texts, or from totally unexpected sources.

 Learning to Pay Attention

When I was first learning Mindell's method of paying attention to flirtations, I found my attention drawn to a soft-

Let your everyday mind become foggy, unknowing, and empty. Try closing your eyes and focusing on your breathing for a few minutes. If you still want to keep track of reading this book, just leave one of your fingers on the spot where you were last reading. When you feel you are ready, begin to slowly open your eyes. Half open them and slowly gaze around. Let your Dreaming mind notice what things flirt with you. If several things catch your attention, let your Dreaming mind choose one of them to focus on. Use your attention to catch this flirt and hold it.

Be patient and loving: notice and stay with what caught your attention. Just be with it. Use your bare attention; hold your focus on it even if it seems meaningless.

Now, see if you can sense the essence of the object that caught your attention, its root or basic tendency or quality. This may be an irrational feeling, but just feel that. Next, experiment with letting that quality unfold. In other words, let it elaborate on itself. Follow its energy, its *ignis,* and its power to unfold. This may be incomprehensible at first. Do not worry about that. Just hold your attention to the powers of that object and watch it unfold itself in terms of feelings, images, and sounds.

—Arnold Mindell, *Dreaming While Awake*[10]

drink vending machine. "Hey," I objected to the universe, "do I have to take this message from a Coke machine?" My sense of self-importance was offended. I could accept that no angel was going to appear, but did I have to listen to something so unspiritual and pedestrian as this?

But it was what was drawing my attention. By staying with it, I found that the message for me was not about Coca-Cola. Instead it was the color red that Coke uses on their machines. For some reason that red was a message to me, a message to be more outgoing and aggressive about what I was doing.

I wouldn't recommend that everyone sit in front of Coke machines waiting for revelations, any more than I'd say that people should go about on arks waiting for doves to bring them olive branches, or wait in caves during storms and earthquakes and fires for a quiet voice. Each of those was a communication at a specific time and place, for a specific person. They were flirtatious invitations to join in communion with a larger reality. By accepting these offers without dismissing them, you also come out of the cave of your separateness and listen.

You'll find that many of the flirtations are invitations to pray for a person or a situation. Someone comes to mind, and there is a feeling of need. You can take this as a sign that you should be praying for that person, and you take a moment to do so. If they come again into your attention, you do it again. Often they will then go, in peace, as if they had come just to get your blessing.

 One Way to Touch

If you like the idea of keeping company but have no idea how to do it, there's help. Patricia Berne, a Catholic lay-woman and psychologist, and Louis Savary, a Catholic priest, some years ago wrote a book called *Kything: the Art of Spiritual Presence.* They took the word from Madeleine L'Engle's *A Wrinkle in Time,* in which an angel uses this old Scots-English word to describe how angels communicate. To kythe is to be present to others spiritually. It is one of the simplest techniques for being in contact with others.

It is a process that is available to all, the authors insist: "Anyone who has a loving heart and acknowledges the reality of the spiritual world can learn to kythe effectively."

HOW TO KYTHE

Get Centered
Count your breaths
Or attend to your body while breathing
Or repeat your name or a mantra with each breath

Focus on the other person
Gaze at them if they are present
Or form an image of them in your mind
Or think of a symbol of them

Establish Connection
"Envision or symbolically image" being present to each other and creating a bond.
Make a choice to create that bond and have it be real.[11]

In their workshops, Savary and Berne found that people could get a sense of other persons at a distance, even of people who are no longer alive. It seems to be part of our human equipment. Savary and Berne also taught people that they could kythe with God, the saints, animals, and trees; and that many people were kything without using the word.

The authors suggest that one should become aware of oneself and of the other as separate persons before they make their union. This is one way to maintain selfhood instead of simply merging into the other. Savary and Berne also mention that if one person does not welcome the kythe it will not happen: "...your spirit seems to go out toward the other but instead of coming to rest there, your spirit seems to bounce back to you as if it had hit a rubber wall."[12] There can be no kything against the will of the participants, and people's secrets seem to be safe as well. If there's something another person does not want known, it will reside behind that rubber wall of privacy.

 Pulsing Together

There are at least two reasons why people do not accept contact with others. Some people wish to preserve their boundaries and privacy, and some people fear an influx of suffering.

Julie Henderson, a Buddhist teacher with a background in somatic psychology and the author of a superb book on the experience of energy,[13] has a strong awareness of boundary issues. She has found that a rich, alive choice, which she calls *pulsation*, exists between rigidity and completely unboundedness. Pulsing allows interaction without breaching the membrane that we sense as our natural container. She teaches her students to pulse softly against other beings and within themselves.

Dr. Henderson has found that it's possible to do the same exercise at a distance, simply by imagining easily and comfortably that you're doing so. The distance vanishes, and the two organisms can pulse against each other as easily as if they were side by side. And whether it is done side by side or at a distance, the pulsing allows both organisms to maintain their boundaries while being in strong energetic contact.

Sometimes experiencing others does bring awareness of their suffering. And for all that it is good to keep company

TOUCHING WITHOUT
GIVING UP BOUNDARIES

Imagine that you are in the presence of the other person.
Imagine that each of you is surrounded by a soft bubble
whose edge is your boundary. Adjust the size of the bubble
until it is exactly as large as you want it to be.

Now move until your bubble just touches that of
the other person. And allow your bubble and theirs to
pulse together, bouncing back and forth softly. Feel the
communication that takes place across your boundaries
without giving them up.   — Julie Henderson

with other people, it is sometimes necessary to pull away
and be alone.

As much as we need ways to be together, we also need
to find ways to mute the contact, to have some silence and
some solitude. The great prophets of Israel went into the
wilderness to be alone. We have the same need.

 Managing Empathy

But if we've opened ourselves to kythe with others, how will
we ever separate ourselves enough to have some quiet in our
souls? After wondering about this for years, I discovered that
many people suffer a sort of involuntary empathy, and that
their coping techniques can work for the rest of us.

"Nadya" came from Europe to the United States. Wherever she lives, she has the same daunting experience:
whatever others around her are feeling, she feels.

She used to feel very much like a manic-depressive, blown about by other people's mood swings. "I thought I was crazy," she says. "My feelings would change suddenly and unpredictably."

She has gradually come to recognize her empathy as a talent as well as an affliction. We talked about her experiences just after she had encountered Rose Rosetree's book for involuntary empaths, *Empowered by Empathy*.[14]

Rosetree emphasizes that before an empath can make use of their skill, they must be able to turn it off. Rosetree has developed techniques to help manage the "Amusement Park" of involuntary empathic experiences. Nadya is learning to separate herself from other people. "I still feel the emotions of other people, but I don't take responsibility for them. I no longer project them on myself — in terms of ownership, or of who is causing them. I establish boundaries, on one level. I try not to close the compassion channel," she said, touching her heart, "But I stop connections if I choose." The feelings of others still come into her; and she may feel them acutely. But if she doesn't want them there, she can simply expel them forcefully from her emotional space.

Natural empaths can learn to manage their own boundaries. They may thicken them a little bit to give themselves some privacy, or they can supervise what comes across those boundaries. In most cases that is enough to provide "a room of one's own." Then it is not necessary to exclude others altogether in order to find some emotional peace.

Increasingly able to manage her own emotional space, Nadya is realizing that her empathic abilities have always allowed her to establish deep connections with people. Even across a continent, she finds, she can both keep company with others and manage the intensity of that contact.

FROM ROSE ROSETREE'S "BREAKING OUT OF THE AMUSEMENT PARK" EXERCISE

...It may take a trip to the bathroom to find privacy, but you'll need only a few minutes to be alone. Pay attention to mood swings, new physical sensations, unusual thinking patterns. Observe without trying to change anything.

Describe in words what it's like for you, being in the Amusement Park right now...ask "What deep, underlying quality do I feel right now?" Allow yourself to receive an answer.

Inwardly ask: "Who am I empathically connected to right now?"...Allow yourself to receive an answer. It could come as a thought, a name, a fragrance, an image. It could flicker by in a flash....

Cut the empathic connection. Say to yourself (aloud if you can) "All that does not belong to me, please leave immediately." It will, because of the immense spiritual power of your free will.

Come Home. Pay attention to what it is like being YOU right now. *Describe it in words...*[15]

 The Communion of Prayer

We keep company with all sorts of beings. We are not only connected with those we pray for, we are also connected with those we pray with. Christians know this connection as "the Communion of Saints," but it is by no means exclusively Christian. When I interviewed the American Muslim Imam Bilal Hyde about the Islamic practice of prayer, he said that praying the ritual prayer (the *salat*) with others immediately connected him with them. "The minute I pray with somebody, you can always tell where they're at, and everybody says this, too, it's not just me."

But it is not only those immediately present that he feels connection with. As he prays the noon prayer, he feels a connection with at least a billion people around the world, of all different races and nationalities, who also pray the daily prayers. "I would describe it as a connectedness," he said. "I don't feel disconnected or released, ever. I never get released, and I hope I never get released! I like the feeling of connectedness!" and he laughed in pleasure.

Only by trying it — by attempting such contact, accepting the subtleties of the touch and the signs of the connection, while maintaining our own boundaries and ending the link when we've had enough — can we find whether this practice of keeping company is for us.

By consciously practicing the connection of keeping company we soon find that we are in a communion of praying people. At one moment we pray for another. At a different moment we ask for prayer. These prayers become the threads that connect us into a tapestry of praying beings. We keep company with others more and more, forever a little bit in contact with all those we have prayed for and those we have prayed with.

THE MOVEMENT OF ENERGY
TOWARD OTHERS

Jesus was on his way through a crowd to the house of Jairus,

> And a certain woman, which had an issue of blood
> twelve years, And had suffered many things of many
> physicians, and had spent all that she had, and was
> nothing bettered, but rather grew worse, When she
> had heard of Jesus, came in the press behind, and
> touched his garment. For she said, If I may touch but
> his clothes, I shall be whole. And straightway the foun-
> tain of her blood was dried up; and she felt in *her* body
> that she was healed of that plague.
>
> And Jesus, immediately knowing in himself that
> virtue had gone out of him, turned him about in the
> press, and said, Who touched my clothes?
> — Mark 5:25–5:30 KJV[16]

Many people alive today know the feeling Jesus was talking
about: Something flows from your body into the body of
the person who needs help. It most often feels like heat. It
moves like a fluid. It seems to stream, rather than moving
in chunks or all at once. It is the "energy" in what is now
called "energy work" or "energetic healing."

I think that it is not supernatural, but natural. All people
have it, some people feel it. Like our voices and our minds,

it is a natural thing we use in praying for others and blessing them.

Energy work is one of the warmest forms of blessing. Life flows out of your hands and moves across to the other person. Whether you touch them physically or not, you can feel the life flowing through you and adding to their life.

Allowing Energy to Flow

There are many varieties of energy treatment. Two of them have spread throughout the world because of skilled teaching and eager promotion by their practitioners, and an interested student can find teachers for both. One is called Reiki, and originated in Japan. The other, Therapeutic Touch, is common among nurses and is taught in some nursing schools.

What exactly is this "energy"? Is it a sort of body-electricity? Is it the stuff of spirit? Is it a bridge between the living and the inanimate, or between spirit and matter? Or is it just an illusion, an impression created by suggestion?

Whatever it is, it's not the result of suggestion. It is not necessary to believe in energy or even to feel it to benefit from energy treatments. The benefit is not a response to the stage-magician-like hand passing near the body. A 1984 study on Therapeutic Touch showed that people almost always respond with relaxation to a TT session, but do not respond so strongly to a fake session in which the hand-passes are made, but in which there is not a healing intention.[17]

If you use Therapeutic Touch on animals, they respond. My neighbor's cat stretches and purrs as I move my hands doing TT over his arthritic hips, but he would whip me with his claws if I touched the sore parts of his body with my hands.

The "energy" may be felt by the practitioner, the patient, by both — or by neither. For those who do feel the energy, the strongest sensation is often a flow of heat. It certainly *feels* like energy. It seems to move from your own hands to the body and environment of the one being treated. Most healers have noticed that the people who are being treated relax. They may sigh or stretch; their muscles may visibly loosen. This is true whether the treatment form involves touch (as Reiki does) or does not have any physical contact (as Therapeutic Touch — surprisingly, given its name — usually does not).

Panta rhei.
"Everything flows."
— Heraclitus

The recipient may not be aware of the feeling of energy, but may notice only the relaxation. If aware of the energy, they will often experience a sense of heat from the healer's hands so strong that it is hard for them to believe that the healer's hands are not very hot. They are surprised when they touch the hands and find them to be normal temperature.

Michael Crichton, M.D. — yes, the author of *Jurassic Park* and *Prey* is a doctor who graduated from Harvard Medical School — has met energy workers and learned to use the energies himself. He wrote: "I lay on the table while the assistants worked on my body. What I noticed was that they would touch a limb at, say, the knee and the ankle. Then, after a minute or two, a sensation of warmth would suddenly spread up and down my lower leg. As soon as that happened, the assistants would go on to another part of the body — say the knee and the hip — and wait until the warmth occurred again. Sometimes this spreading warmth was accompanied by a little twitch in the limb, but usually not. In any case, the assistants seemed able to tell when the warmth began, because they immediately moved to another part of my body. As more and more of my body was treated in this way, I drifted into a deep relaxation close to sleep."[18]

The heat may originally be felt only where the hands are placed. In many cases it then moves away from the hands, seeking those places that most need help. I can recall when I was receiving Reiki as part of the first course I took. The person working on me placed her hands on my upper back, and it felt as if her hands were heating pads. Then the heat formed itself into a ball, and moved down my back to my lower back, which is often stiff and vulnerable. The Reiki-giver's hands remained on my shoulders; I felt the energy from them sixteen inches away near the base of my spine.

At the end of a session, the recipient often feels both re-laxed and recharged. Specific areas of pain may have eased. Sometimes there are remarkable healings, but at a mini-mum, stress is greatly reduced. And most of all, people feel touched, noticed, and held.

Generations of energy-workers have discovered that it is not wise to use your *own* energy. Chinese Qi Gong heal-ers traditionally charge themselves with energy before they begin. Reiki healers work with "universal energy" that flows through them. One of the reasons that Reiki is transmitted with an initiation, in fact, is to open the body's receiving and sending abilities so that energy can pass through. A person who gives Reiki to another usually comes away feeling more charged, not depleted.

If you are foolish enough to use your own energy, it can be frighteningly draining. I visited a friend of mine in the convalescent hospital. I was just a beginner. He was very sick, and very receptive to energy work. As I gave energy, he accepted it. He kept on accepting it, and kept on; and I felt myself growing weaker and weaker. Finally I had to excuse myself. I left the convalescent home and went to a restaurant where I ate a full meal in a fortunately successful attempt to recharge myself. And I never again used my own energy to work on anyone.

> An analogy to this healing process can be found in physics. If one connects two identical vessels together, each of which contains water at a different height, the siphoning process will allow the water level in the two containers to be at the same height. Similarly this would occur to the energy field of persons doing healing if they were not connected to the intuitional field. Their energy level would be drained by the patient. However as long as the healer is a channel, through which the healing energy flows, he/she does not use his/her own energy. The healer's level during this siphon process is continuously replenished....
>
> —Dora Kunz and Erik Peper[19]

Cultures around the world connect Wind, Life-Energy and Breath. Christian healers frequently invite the Holy Ghost to come into them; two of the commonest manifestations of the Holy Spirit are energetic: a great wind, and tongues of fire. The Spirit of God exists in both Jewish and Islamic thought, and in both cultures the word for Spirit means Wind. The Spirit of God moves over the face of the waters at the beginning of the Torah, and in the next chapter the Lord breathes the breath of life into Adam. One of the meanings of *prana* in Sanskrit is breath. In Tibetan medicine, a hybrid of Chinese and Indian views, the word for energy of this sort is simply "wind."

In both India and China the connection has been elaborated into elaborate medical models in which life energy is brought in as breath and circulates through channels in the body. When there's enough of it in the right place, you're healthy. When the energy is stopped or depleted, you're sick. When it is missing entirely, you're dead.

The energy is found not only within us but also around us; and we can draw on that larger reservoir. If you invite the benevolent energy of the universe to flow through you, the power you use is both kind and unlimited. For those who experience the energy, it is easy to believe it is the breath of life, given to us in the Garden. That's why we find energetic laying on of hands to be one of the most common forms of blessing for others — we are giving life itself.

 ## *The Practice of Spirit Energy*

"Reiki" in Japanese means Spirit Energy. It arose early in the last century in Japan, a time, like our own, of rapid social change. Practitioners of Reiki have heard many variations of the story of its founding by Mikao Usui: that he was a Christian, a Spiritualist, or a Buddhist, that he went to America to find how to perform Christian miracles, or that he did not. In 1922 he did retire to Mt. Kurama to fast, pray, and read Buddhist sutras. At the end of twenty-one days a light came to him. When he recovered consciousness, he was able to heal by the laying on of hands.[20] All accounts agree that he taught the system, and that it was brought to North America by a Japanese-American woman, Hawayo Takata.[21] Reiki also continues in several lineages in Japan.

Reiki is not just learned; it is transmitted. Students are taught by teachers who also initiate them and open their energy channels to do the work. The teachers were themselves initiated by others in a (theoretically) unbroken succession going back to Usui.

Basic Reiki as taught by Takata consists of laying hands on a client. This distinguishes it from some forms of energy work in which you work "in the aura," near the body, without actually touching the client. The recipient is usually lying on a massage table, fully clothed and often with eyes closed. The Reiki practitioner places both hands first on the head, and then works down the body of the recipient. Eyes, ears, the back of the head, mid-chest, mid-back, lower back, upper abdomen, lower abdomen, knees, and feet are common places to rest the hands. The hands are allowed to remain for a period of time at each location, while the Reiki energy passes through the practitioner and into the body of the recipient. Reiki practitioner and teacher Priscilla Stuckey says that the energy seems to flow through her head, body, and hands, and then out her arms.[22]

The hands may be left in the same place for two to several minutes until there is a feeling of fullness or sufficiency, or at least until the appropriate amount of time has passed. Then the practitioner moves the hands to the next of the customary positions.

Reiki teachers all emphasize that it is the recipient, not the Reiki practitioner, who regulates the flow of energy. The recipient accepts the energy in exactly the amount and type needed, and then (when "full") declines to take any more. I would have found this difficult to accept until I experienced it both as the recipient and as a giver of the energy. The practitioner gets a sensation of "enough," which I felt as a kind of back-pressure; the energy just didn't flow any more. Dr. Stuckey says she goes by how her hands feel, with

> When the radio station broadcasts, there are no lines connected from the station to your house, yet as you turn on the receiver and contact the station, you receive what they are sending. Because we are not radio technicians, we do not know how. The principles are the same with Reiki. This energy goes through space without wires, and we know this great force can be contacted. Once the contact is made, the energy flow is automatic. It is universal, limitless energy. When you have the switch on, the power is unlimited. When you want to stop, you just take your hands away. It is very simple. — Dr. Chujiro Hayashi[23]

a three- to five-minute time limit in each position. Sometimes, she says, she feels nothing. "Other times I definitely feel something happening, the hands will heat up, you feel the heat rise, it stays at high temperature for a while, then it goes down and relaxes again. Then I move on."

Reiki initiators teach the practitioners some hand gestures called "symbols" to increase the energy flow. I have used them; I cannot say for sure if they do increase or change the flow. But what does change the flow is the person you're working with. One draws a warm flow, another a cool and cleansing flow; a third wants and gets a hot, reviving energy. It is as if something within the person places an order, and you're just the delivery channel.

To a large extent Reiki has moved through what used to be called the Alternative Culture. I learned it from a New Age musician, for instance. It has no essential connection with the New Age; in fact a Polish nun received permission from the Pope to practice the art.[24] The primary experience of giving and receiving Reiki is a peace that does not argue doctrine. In the words of Priscilla Stuckey: "That Reiki silence, that Reiki calm, descended on the room, where everything is in tune, and everything is all right."

 The Use of Therapeutic Touch

Some people want something that fits easily into scientific or technical environments. Some nursing schools across the country teach a form of energy work called Therapeutic Touch. One of the founders of Therapeutic Touch was Dolores Krieger, Ph.D., R.N., Professor of Nursing at New York University. Teachers of Therapeutic Touch have been careful to seek neutral and scientific language, in an occasionally successful attempt to make TT acceptable within standard medicine.

Therapeutic Touch involves smoothing and untangling the energy fields that surround the body. In a five-step process, practitioners begin by meditatively *centering* themselves. Then, by running hands slowly over the surface of the body at a distance of about four to six inches from the surface, the practitioner *assesses* the condition of the patient and may receive impressions of heat, density, or tangledness. The practitioner will *clear and mobilize* the recipient's energy field, which has the effect of relaxing and opening the field. Then come *specific interventions* — perhaps to comb out a tangle or to add energy to an area that seems depleted. Finally the field is *rebalanced, smoothed, and closed* with long passes, and the practitioner releases contact with the patient.[25]

This practice is so reminiscent of the magnetic passes of Anton Mesmer that it stirs ancestral memories in the guardians of medicine's secularity. Nevertheless, it works. Refereed journals of nursing have published a number of careful studies. According to one: "To date, these studies, which control for placebo effects, have provided initial evidence that TT may decrease anxiety, decrease pain, increase function in osteoarthritic joints, increase a sense of well-being, joy, vitality and peace, and decrease the amount of pain medication used following surgery."[26]

Although many recipients and practitioners of Therapeutic Touch "feel something," you don't have to have any experience of energy to be an effective practitioner. Janet Quinn, R.N., Ph.D., and a Fellow of the American Academy of Nursing, has been doing, teaching, and researching Therapeutic Touch for many years. But since she first encountered the method in a class taught by Dr. Krieger, she has almost never *felt* the energy herself. She does occasionally get "impressions," as do a number of other practitioners of TT, revealing that the style of perception varies in this as in other forms of prayer and blessing for others.

The Paradox of Energy Work

An energy — like electricity, which also has healing properties — could serve as a bridge between the physical sciences and spiritual practices.

The energy used in this form of blessing presents itself experientially as something very much like heat. When it is flowing, the practitioner often feels warmth in the hands. The recipient is very likely to feel heat at the same time. Some people see it as well — I never have — as a glow that surrounds the body. How could it not be energy, in the ordinary sense of the word?

Nevertheless, the energy has not been found. Therapeutic Touch practitioner and researcher Janet Quinn says that the existence of a human energy field has not yet been

> There is no simple answer to the question "Who is doing the healing?" Is it the innate healing potential within all living things? Is it the life energy, a universal force that has order as its basis? Is it the practitioner, who serves as a conduit or an instrument? Or is it a combination of all three at a crucial moment? I have tried to explain what I understand about assisting the healing process through Therapeutic Touch, but essentially it remains a mystery, as does life itself.
>
> — Janet Macrae, *Therapeutic Touch: A Practical Guide*

demonstrated through Western science, and so the concept remains scientifically theoretical.[27] Michael Crichton wrote that the energies can be felt and seen, and that they are connected to health and healing, but that Western medicine does not yet accept them. He guesses that when Western medicine *does* accept these energies, it will at the same time understand once again the importance of bedside manner, hand-holding, and the art in medicine.[28]

One reason that the scientific world has had trouble accepting this energy is that it works as well at a distance as it does in person. You can direct it several feet, or across a great distance, and the same results follow as if you were working on a person right in front of you.

In its second-degree initiation Reiki teaches people how to do distant treatment with Reiki energy. Practitioners often use a pillow or even a stuffed toy as a surrogate for the one being treated. Priscilla Stuckey once treated a sick deer who was uncharacteristically lying for hours near a road at mid-day. She worked on the doe indirectly by "mocking her up" on a pillow. After she treated the distant animal for a short time, she felt that the problem had dissipated. She put down the pillow and looked again; the doe had gotten to her feet and was gone.

Energies in the physical sciences attenuate over distance. The energies involved in energetic blessing seem not to.

They also respond to thought. "Energy follows attention" is a motto in a number of energy-based practices. So a practitioner learns that it's possible to do energy-blessings without using the hands at all, though using the hands remains the easiest way to work.

The energy also seems to have an intelligence of its own. You can do energy work on someone and never know what's wrong, yet the energy will go to the place that needs it most, do its work, and then stop flowing when the work is done. If the patient has just enough faith to *permit* it to work, it will help.

Energy as a Guide

When you begin a session of Therapeutic Touch, after centering yourself, you assess the field of the person you're working with. Some people find it a novel experience to "feel the energy" of another person; others will recognize it immediately as something they've done all their lives. They may have a private language with which they describe it: "I get a nice feeling from this place." "I sense he is not well." "She seems jangled, but nice."

One way to recognize energetic perception is that it often feels *environmental*, as if the area around the person has this quality. In fact experienced energy blessers report that places do have discernible energies, so that it is appropriate to pray for a "where" as well as for a "who."

> Lord, make me an instrument of your peace,
> Where there is hatred, let me sow love;
> ...where there is injury, pardon;
> ...where there is doubt, faith;
> ...where there is despair, hope;
> ...where there is darkness, light;
> ...where there is sadness, joy...
>
> —from the Prayer of St. Francis

If you're one of those who have always felt energy, you can use it as guide. Even if you never project or channel energy to a person or an environment, feeling the "vibe" in their presence can tell you how to pray for them. Do you feel leaden and slow around them? Then you might pray that they will experience aliveness. Do you feel anger? Then offer peace. Your awareness of the energy in a place allows you to insert other qualities into the field, drawing on the universal field to do so.

The Intimacy of Energy Work

There is a warmth and involvement in doing energy work with someone else. In a culture that is largely touch-deprived, so that people feel lonely in their skins all the time, energy work can be kindness.

At the same time, just as some people do not like to be touched physically, some people do not like to be touched energetically. It is both wise and kind to respect that desire. Always ask if it is OK to touch someone; if you are working inside someone's energy, it is worthwhile to ask energetically as well.

Once I was working with a woman from India. I asked her verbally if it was all right to touch her, and she said, "Yes." At the same time her energy said "No!" with a resonance of the very ancient modesty of India, in which man simply does not touch a woman casually.

Energy is the first step outside of the bounds of the body.

— Julie Henderson

I chose to believe her energy. I said something like "Hmm, it feels as if your energy would prefer I don't touch you. Might I work on the edge of your field?" She relaxed visibly; and verbally *and* energetically, she said yes. So I combed the edge of her field, more than a foot away from her skin, and she grew composed, comfortable, and centered. If I had believed her words instead of her energy, I think we both would have had an uncomfortable time.

Energy presents itself as a concrete and "ordinary" thing. It seems so very much like a massage that it doesn't require much faith to use it. For many people it is a beginning in their practice of blessing, a "first step," as Dr. Henderson says. Yet it can go far, reach distant people and situations, and sometimes accomplish very deep healings. If the practice of a silent, warm form of blessing appeals to you, energy work may be your calling. It allows you to connect with the recipient without words, and give comfort and healing.

ASKING FOR HELP FROM OTHERS

In the middle of the afternoon my wife, Nancy, got a call. Neighbors wanted her to come over because they knew that she was a social worker. Their twelve-year-old daughter's friend was having severe stomach pains. The neighbor suspected it was more than sickness. She thought the child was in labor, and she was right.

Together we rushed the girl to the hospital. She was admitted. We contacted her conservative immigrant parents, from whom she had managed to conceal her pregnancy. "Get rid of it," said her mother. But it was too late: the girl was about to give birth to a full-term baby. The child of a child, the baby would be born unwanted into an unwelcoming family.

While the girl was in labor, the only thing I knew how to do was to call Silent Unity. The New Thought/Christian Unity Church that publishes Daily Word also operates a twenty-four-hour prayer ministry from its headquarters near Kansas City. The prayer worker listened while I described the circumstances, and then in a compassionate voice with a Missouri twang, she prayed for two children she would never see.

The baby was born healthy, and the young mother was well despite her attempt to conceal her pregnancy by starving herself. But what was to become of the new child?

Within a few days, the family of the father (also twelve years old) decided to adopt the child and raise him as their own.

I'm sorry to say that I never told Silent Unity the outcome of their prayers: The mother would be able to see her child occasionally, and the new baby boy was welcomed into a family of his own culture. But there was no doubt in my mind that the prayers of strangers had helped this child find a home.

 ## Praying With and For Others

Orthodox Judaism requires that a *minyan,* a group of ten, gather for prayers. Buddhists "take refuge" in the Samgha, the community of Buddhists. Christianity relies on Jesus' saying: " . . . if two of you shall agree on earth as touching any thing that they shall ask, it shall be done for them of my Father which is in heaven. For where two or three are gathered together in my name, there am I in the midst of them."[29]

I believe that people in every culture that prays also ask others to pray for them. "Pray your best prayer for me," says a Muslim as he departs from friends. That practice is the basis of this book as well: the belief that we can and should pray for each other.

There is something special about joining with others in prayer. You can be very cynical or shy about prayer, but the moment you ask others to pray for someone specific that you care about, all the grief and hope that goes into prayer bubbles to the surface.

For many years I have had the privilege of working with an online Buddhist prayer group. Every day people send in requests that are forwarded to the 150 members. The asking and the responding add something to our lives. The person who asked is no longer alone with their need, and the person who responds is able to help. A community is created; and that, I think, that is the very first answer to prayer.

But it is not the only one. Over the years that I've been involved with our prayer group, my impression is that a large number of the requests are realized. Not all, by any means, but many. It's as if the attention from others is somehow more effective than one's own prayers, and good wishes heap up to make good things happen.

Marion von Gienanth, a German member of our group, told about interventions — she is not sure prayer is the right word — by her Zen teacher. When Marion was so sick with bronchitis that she was coughing blood, her Zen master Brigitte Koun An D'Ortschy worked on her without telling her. Within a few minutes Marion's chest was free and open. The Zen master had worked on her by just touching a leaf that Marion had given her.

Five years later her three-year-old son was very sick with shingles. Marion was scared and called her for help. The Zen master was teaching at that time, and said that she would take care of him later. About noon the child suddenly opened his eyes, sat up, and started to play as if nothing were wrong with him. This was exactly the time when the Zen teacher concentrated on him. "Nobody in the clinic could believe it," says Marion.

 Finding a Prayer Group

Fundamentalist Christians have created our cultural model of a prayer group. A few people gather together and take turns asking for specific needs and specific people. The others in the group then join them in asking God to grant help to those who need it.

This is such a perfect way to pray that I wish all communities would adopt it. I know that our group has. In addition to our online prayer group, some of us meet occasionally to work together. At the beginning of the day we make a list of the people and situations we want to work for. We take a moment to hold each intention and perhaps surround it with mantra and "wisdom presence," because this is how we pray. Then, just like the Christians, we frequently get guidance about how we should change our prayer, and we do so. Someone in heaven must have a sense of humor, for a Buddhist group in California to imitate a Fundamentalist Christian group.

Many churches have prayer groups that may welcome people from outside their own immediate congregation. There are also interdenominational groups such as the Order of St. Luke, a Christian lay-order devoted to praying for the sick.[30]

Just to go to church, mosque, synagogue, or temple is to join a prayer group. Many Protestant congregations have midweek prayer and healing services, and Orthodox Jews frequently attend synagogue daily. Roman Catholic churches have special group prayer ceremonies: a rosary is said for the dead before a funeral, and novenas — nine-day ceremonies that are dedicated to the attending person's intention — are frequent in more traditional churches. Attendance at such programmed prayer events lets you join others in prayer without having to say your intention — that can be a blessing for the very shy. Churches, synagogues, mosques, and temples also have clergy who will pray with you.

But the small group and the formal religious organization are by no means the only ways to pray with others. Online prayer groups can create a real community for their participants and allow people to have a prayer group that meets at any hour of the day or night in a chat room. We use a mailing list, so people can pick up their email and join the prayer when they can get to their computer.

Prayer is at the heart of Silent Unity, and prayer is a heart-to-heart connection that links all people spiritually with each other and with God. This spirituality, which transcends all religions, represents a oneness — a unity. And we can best access this spiritual unity through the silence of prayer.

— Silent Unity website

A number of large religious organizations that offer telephone prayer help have also created online prayer request web sites. Silent Unity has been taking telephone requests (816-969-2000, TDD 816-525-1155, Spanish 816-969-2020) ever since the telephone became common. As computers have spread throughout the world, the group has also begun accepting prayer requests online at *www.unityworldhq.org/silent_unity.htm.* Religious Science's World Ministry of Prayer has a website at *www.wmop.org* and invites prayer requests by email; or at 800-421-9600 (from within the United States or Canada), 720-284-6956 (from all other countries), or by fax at 213-637-0711. The Well (*www.well.com*) has been an online community and discussion-haunt since the 1980s. In its news conference, there is always a topic called "Wellbeams," or lately just "beams," in which members ask with no theological presuppositions at all for prayers for themselves and others.

The point is that when you are praying for someone, you do not ever have to pray alone.

The Three Faces of Prayer

All of us who pray have a triple role: We pray for help for others and ourselves, we join others and pray with them, and we are ourselves prayed to.

"Huh?" says the reasonable person, failing to see candles before their shrine. But if someone asks us for money, asks for food, or asks that we pray our best prayer for them, they are praying to us.

Sometimes the person speaks or writes to us, but sometimes they reach out silently. If we are aware of this kind of cry, we respond as if we had been asked in person. The contact is just as real. Parents often feel it. So do spiritual teachers.

American Protestant Glenn Clark reported being kept awake by a silent plea from one of his students. He suddenly felt a great sense of oppression, as if someone were trying to reach him. He prayed that evening and the following morning without receiving any peace. On Sunday evening he prayed again, with other believers, "And this time a great peace came to me."

The next day a student came to his office and asked if he had "gotten her message." She had been visiting friends, and their child had been very sick. In her uncertainty she had called out for Clark's help.

Clark suggested that she call the family. When the girl did so, she found that the child had passed the crisis on Sunday evening, and the family had been able to dismiss the trained nurse.[31]

The silent request for help to a living Sheikh is so common among Muslim Sufis that it has its own name. Sufi Imam Bilal Hyde explains that the Arabic word is *Nida'*. "That means calling upon people. Just invoking their presence, in order for them to immediately help, through God's omnipotence, that they help immediately. It's like a red telephone calling upon someone," said Hyde.

Empaths in particular grow used to being silently invited to pray for complete strangers or distant situations. Because the experience is contrary to the larger culture's understanding they rarely talk about it, but when they gather they often discuss the varieties of silent appeal. One person is aware of how bodies are suffering, and the help they need. Another is aware of social groups. A third is aware of a huge group, the stock market. Others feel the anguish of regions in conflict, and pray for peace. One said of praying for Israel and Palestine, "It feels like the earth in the Holy Land is twisted with anger and pain, and can get no ease. I pray that it rest, and its people be able to rest too."

In each case the situation calls out to us, as if it were praying to us; and we try to respond.

Religions that forbid idolatry would have to wonder if these "prayers" to us, and our prayers to others, are worship. My answer would be just no. When we call on someone else for help, we are honoring them as powerful and helpful. But we are not worshipping them, any more than we worship the staff of the emergency room when we receive medical treatment. We come to them because they are skilled, good-willed, and willing. We may be deeply in need and profoundly grateful, but we do not worship them.

 ## The Promises of the Saints

I've never understood why some communities whose members cheerfully ask each other for prayer stop asking people for their prayers after they've died. After all, those who have died are believed to be closer to God — assuming that they died well, of course — and are therefore in an even better position to ask for help.

Orthodox and Catholic Christianity, on the other hand, often ask the holy departed for their prayers. They call them saints. Mahayana Buddhists ask for the assistance of bodhisattvas, heroic individuals who have vowed to spend as many lives as necessary to free all beings. The popularity of angels testifies to the presence of helpful spirits, and Spiritualism is based on the assistance one can receive from the friendly departed. The Day of the Dead among Mexicans (and increasingly among non-Latinos as well) honors those who have died, prays with and for them, and affirms that death does not break our connection with them.

Hail Mary, full of grace, the Lord is with thee. Blessed art thou amongst women, and blessed is the fruit of thy womb, Jesus. Holy Mary, Mother of God, pray for us sinners now and at the hour of our death. Amen.   — The *Ave Maria*

Even austerely monotheistic religions have de facto saints. Muslims who might have called out to a sheikh while that worthy was alive will often visit the tomb of a departed sheikh to pray; and Muslims tell tales of interventions by Khidr, whom the West calls St. George. Judaism too has saints. Elijah intervenes in the lives of the faithful from time to time, and comes through the opened door on Passover. Lubavitcher Chassidim[32] have been known to ask the departed rebbe for his intervention.

All that is necessary to ask for help is — to ask for help. That is, to turn your mind to the saint you are addressing, and say what you want. You can use a traditional prayer, or just ask conversationally. Then you can go about your business. For most people there is no visible or audible response — but conditions change.

Forgive me for putting it this way, but saints seem to serve as an acceptable retailer of Holiness. If you had to do business with the president of a large company, would you rather do it trembling in person, or use the good offices of someone close to that president and also to you? In prayer, these intermediaries are the saints: They are not the Ultimate themselves, but our fellow creatures who assist us to contact that Holiness, and to whom we go willingly for help because they seem easy to approach. They offer three things to us as their fellow beings: *company, help,* and *uplift.*

The Promise of Company

First, they keep company with us. No matter how alone we feel, they offer to be with us. We will not face the sufferings of life alone, they say; we have them at our side.

Jesus asked this of his disciples — "Watch with me"[33] — when he went to pray in the garden of Gethsemane. He didn't ask for their intercession or their help — just that they stay with him.

The Promise of Help

Then the saints offer us help. If we are lost in a snowstorm, they will help us find shelter. If we're poor, they will help us find a job and a house and food. If we're sick, they will help us heal.

For many of us this is the great question, the heart, of prayer: Is there help? And the consensus of religions around the world is that yes, there is. These beings have committed to help us. Much of the doctrinal dispute in religion is about which being you can trust and which you may ask for assistance; but all religions agree that the help is there for us.

Thanks to the Blessed Mother, St. Anthony, and St. Jude. D.R.

— Classified ad, *St. Louis Post-Dispatch*
10/30/2002 — 11/02/2002

Sometimes the help is unasked for and has no theological label.

Harry Monahan was a submariner in World War II and a fine television cameraman in his later years. But the disease that put him in the hospital almost killed him. He was in for a long time, very weak. He began to look forward to the visit of "the hippie girl," a candy-striper who visited him almost every day. She laughed and kept him company, and helped restore his will to live.

Finally he recovered, and as his family came to take him home he asked to say goodbye to "the hippie girl." But no one on the staff had heard of her and no one, except Harry, had seen her. And Harry never forgot her.[34]

The Promise of Uplift

Many of these traditions offer a further promise: the helpers can lift us up so that we can join them. We too can become helpers to others. This is what lies at the base of the intercessory prayer vocation: we ask for help for others, and in doing so we join the helping beings.

All the traditions who have saints also tell of great sinners who become holy beings. St. Paul began by persecuting the same community for which he would later evangelize. St. Dismas, "The Good Thief," was being executed for his crimes when he spoke up for Jesus and entered the Kingdom of Heaven. The Buddha's disciple Angulimala had previously been a killer, collecting human fingers for a gruesome rosary (his name means "rosary of fingers"). He was converted by the Buddha and later became the patron invoked during painful childbirth.

Because I am poor, I pray for every living creature.
— Kiowa Indian[35]

The promise of uplift applies not only to the already virtuous. It applies also, and especially, to those who have great sins on their conscience.

 ## *Help from Saints*

If it is so important to work with these helpful beings, how does one find one? Sometimes images of saints or bodhisattvas draw you. St. Jude, the patron of impossible cases (and, as my mother says, "of impossible people") is one such for me. So is good St. Anne, the mother of Mary and the grandmother of Christ; and Th'röma, the black Vajrayogini of spaciousness. Why do these saints draw me to them? I don't know; I never have known.

It's like the affinity between people. Anyone who has ever tried to matchmake for friends knows just how mysterious affinity can be. But one sign of affinity is, well, affinity: if you're drawn to a saint, try calling out to them and asking for help in the life of the spirit. These are beings who have made themselves available to us for just this connection, to pray with us when we pray for others. The ally who appears may be a surprise, but they seem to match our temperaments.

And sometimes you'll be drawn to different saints for different prayers. I find that when I ask for help with my brother-in-law, St. Francis comes to mind. And when I ask St. Francis to keep an eye on my brother-in-law, I feel certain things: a sense of presence, like the feeling that someone is with me, and a flavor to that presence that marks it as someone specific. It is not just anyone, it is *someone*. From keeping company with people at a distance, I've learned to trust that flavor-sensation as the mark of a real person.

And I feel a sense of reassurance: I don't know what to do about my brother-in-law, but there's a feeling that if St. Francis is on the case, things are OK. In no way do I worship St. Francis; if anything I may be a little too straightforward in my fellowship with him. But he and I share an interest in my brother-in-law, and I am glad for that.

 ## *Help for Every Purpose under Heaven*

If no saint speaks to you intuitively, every tradition has catalogues that connect saints and purposes. Two of my favorites are the tongue-in-cheek book about Catholic saints by Kelly and Rogers, *Saints Preserve Us!*,[36] and the somewhat more serious *Meeting the Buddhas*[37] about Buddhist saints.

Those who do laundry, for instance, can pray to St. Veronica, who wiped Jesus' face on the way to the Crucifixion. Musicians and composers remember St. Cecilia, inventor of the organ. St. Phocas is a patron of gardeners and (because his name is similar to the Greek and Breton words for "seal") of those who go to sea as well. St. Clare of Assisi is the patron of television — she saw a vision of Christmas on her wall in her old age. Mañjushri is a Buddhist bodhisattva concerned with scholarship and all matters intellectual, along with the luminously beautiful gold-skinned bodhisattva of wisdom, Prajñaparamita. Dzambhala, with his mongoose who spits jewels, helps those who seek wealth.

> Blessed Cecilia appear in visions
> To all musicians, appear and inspire:
> Translated daughter, come down and startle
> Composing mortals with immortal fire.
> —W. H. Auden, *Anthem on St. Cecilia's Day*

St. Jude prays for those with impossible cases. St. Anthony helps find lost objects. St. Joseph helps people to sell their real estate. St. Bueno (Welsh, not Spanish) and St. Brighid both care for cattle. Tara the bodhisattva is called *turā*, the "eager one," and portrayed with one foot down from her meditation in her readiness to come to the aid of those who ask for her help. St. Maximilian Kolbe, a priest who in Auschwitz volunteered to die in the place of another prisoner and was executed by lethal injection, is patron of those struggling with drugs. Jizo (the Japanese name for Kshitigarbha) cares for children, particularly those lost in miscarriage or abortion, and his shrines in Japan are filled with tiny statues wearing baby clothes.

Regions have their patron saints. Mary, as the Virgin of Guadalupe, is patron of Mexico. St. Denis (St. Dionysus) has long been a patron of France, where, say Kelly and Rogers: "After Our Saint was decapitated in the somewhat unsavory Montmartre district, he picked up his head and carried it six miles to the present site of the great cathedral that bears his name. 'The first step,' said the Saint's head, 'was the difficult one.' "

St. Anne is a patron of Canada. She was also a favorite of Martin Luther, so she might make a good patron for Protestants. Tara, in her sixteen-year-old green form, is patron of Tibet, while in her mature form as White Tara she is patron of Mongolia. Padmasambhava, one of the Buddhist missionaries to Tibet, is a patron of the many places in Nepal, Sikkim, and Tibet, where he visited and meditated — his handprint is found in a cave wall near Kathmandu. Machig Labdrön is patroness of all the desolate places, where her fierce and generous *chöd* visualization rite of feeding all beings with one's own body is practiced by *chödmas* and *chödpas*.

Kuan Yin is a patron of compassion. Female in China, Korea, Vietnam, and Japan, she is also the male bodhisattva Avalokiteshvara in Indian, Nepal, and Tibet, therefore s/he is a patron for all who have complicated genders. St. Jerome was famous for his irascibility, and he has appealed to angry people ever since. So do the many "wrathful" bodhisattvas of tantric Buddhism, who convert the energy of anger into the energy of compassion and enlightenment. Women's sexuality in Christianity is (quite unofficially and quite universally) the province of St. Mary Magdalen, and in Buddhism of the Vajrayoginis who dance naked. St. Thomas is forever the patron for those of us who doubt, and therefore probably of Unitarians. St. Christina the Astonishing had near-death and out-of-body experiences, and is patron of psychiatrists. For gritty humor under fire, the patron must be St. Lawrence: while being martyred by being grilled alive on an iron griddle, he said to his torturer, "Turn me over; I'm done on this side." Yes, he *is* the patron of cooks.

 ## A Wrong Saint?

Jean Vianney was a nineteenth-century French curate who was famous as a confessor. He heard confessions fourteen to eighteen hours a day, a task that is the equivalent of doing therapy that many hours. He was unquestionably a holy man, and people traveled from all over France to be shriven and advised by him. He was also completely devoted to St. Philomena, a young martyr of Roman times whose bones had been discovered at the beginning of the nineteenth century.

But it now appears that, while Jean Vianney's sanctity was real, his patron saint may not have been. The Catholic Church has removed her feast from the liturgical calendar. If she was legendary, we have the paradox that a real saint became holy (and many other miracles were wrought) through the intervention of a fictitious saint. The only reasonable conclusion is that the Holy receives all prayers, and that Krishna's words in the *Bhagavad Gita* are accurate:

> Even those who worship other gods,
> Sacrificing with faith,
> Also sacrifice to Me . . . [38]

If despite modern scholarly opinion and Vatican caution St. Philomena was real after all, she must surely be the patron of those who worry whether their prayers are properly directed — but pray anyway.

When we pray with others, embodied or not, we take advantage of the Communion of Saints, the *Samgha*, that links all those of good intention. In this view, the very fact of praying for others sincerely makes anyone — for that moment — a saint and part of the vast conspiracy of good will that prayer for others creates. The experience of being able to reach across time and space means that our prayer group can include those who are expected or unexpected, near or far, dead or alive or yet unborn. They are eager to help. It would be folly not to draw on their assistance.

FOLLOWING DIVINE GOALS
AND METHODS

When Nona's sister Lavinia began to hemorrhage again, Nona was near the edge of despair. Lavinia might bleed for hours. It was late nineteenth-century Colorado, and calling a doctor was expensive for a poor family. It was the desperation that drove her to try the "treatment" that she had learned in a class about newfangled, heretical metaphysical healing. "God is everywhere, therefore God is here. God is health. Health is everywhere. Therefore health is here. Lavinia cannot be ill..." she began, tentatively using the words she had never used before. And it was certainly desperate need that made her keep on, past all common sense and the obvious fact that Lavinia *was* ill.

"God is her health. God is her health. God is her health!"

She could never heal anyone. Then, suddenly, it came to her. God could heal anyone. It was no longer a thought or an affirmation, it was just *so*.

"What do you want? Here is the power. What do you want?"

She wanted that Lavinia be healed. And with a tiny shift, it was done.

She heard her brother racing downstairs with the news: Lavinia's bleeding had stopped. It would never happen again. And Nona would grow up to be Nona Brooks, a founder of the Church of Divine Science.[39]

 Two Sorts of Prayer

"Metaphysical" churches have taken the idea that Mind creates and made it the center of their prayer practice. In particular, they apply that idea to make life good in *this* world. In the words of W. Frederic Keeler: "In Truth and in Christian Victory we refuse to accept soul-saving as an institution of God and at the same time admit starvation and lack and bodily loss in His name."[40]

And the earth was without form, and void; and darkness [was] upon the face of the deep. And the Spirit of God moved upon the face of the waters.

And God said, Let there be light: and there was light.

—Genesis 1:2–3 KJV

The emphases in the different Metaphysical views produce different themes in Metaphysical healing; practitioners mix these in different proportions in their treatments. One — "Belief creates" — is common among New Thought churches like Religious Science, Unity, Divine Science, and Japan's Seicho no Ie. Another theme, stronger in Christian Science, is that each being has a spiritual identity created by God. If we contemplate and love that identity, that being will manifest the innate perfection it already possesses.

Belief Creates

Those who emphasize "Belief creates" see a universe that is fundamentally malleable. It has no shape of its own, except the shape that Spirit gives it. The malleability means that creation is not finished, but continues forever. The Mind of God is always making the universe, and the universe's Law is to be responsive to that Mind.

> Child, you are always with me,
> And all that I have is yours.
> —Luke 15:31[41]

What is true of the universe, they assert, is true of each individual. There is a tradition in both the West and Asia that God is the prototype, and we are made in the image of God. From this many have concluded that the same ability to say "Let there be . . . ," by which God created the Universe, also exists in us. As God made images in divine thought and they came to exist, so do we create with our minds.

> One of the most fascinating things which you will ever learn is that this Law, which exists at the center of your being, is creative; that you use the same creativeness which brought the planets into being, the same creativeness which produces everything that is. . . . When you speak, it speaks within you. Thus your thought becomes the law of your life because the Law of One Mind already resides at the center of your being.   —Ernest Holmes[42]

If we create our own reality, why do we suffer? Those Metaphysicals who prefer the "Belief Creates" theme say that we cause our own suffering by thinking wrongly. We give images of lack and pain to the Universal Law, and it obediently produces them in our experience.

As Ernest Holmes says, "Ever since you have had self-conscious thought, you have, by your use of the law of liberty, created bondage. Not that bondage ever really existed, but the possibility of using freedom in a limited way existed. You never really BOUND freedom, you merely used it in a RESTRICTED way. The restriction was not in the Principle, but in your use of it."[43]

Therefore I say unto you, What things soever ye desire, when ye pray, believe that ye receive them, and ye shall have them.
— Mark 11:24 KJV

Those who focus on the theme "Belief Creates" maintain that if your universe is unsatisfactory, you should change your beliefs. It may not be easy to change belief when all the evidence supports the old thoughts, and there is no support yet for the new vision. But it can be accomplished: " . . . by combining belief, emotion, and imagination, and forming them into a mental picture of the desired physical result. Of course, the wanted result is not yet physical or you would not need to create it, so it does no good to say your physical experience seems to contradict what you are trying to do."[44]

For many healers the state in which they start to treat is anything but believing and joyous. The story that begins this chapter is from a biography of Nona Brooks, a founder of Divine Science. There is doubt and fear, but persistence in the treatment. Then the words that were a desperate affirmation give way to an experienced reality. The "click of acceptance" is the subjective sign that the healing has taken place. Returning to ordinary experience, the healer finds that "it is done." The mere words in an affirmation have become experienced-reality, and the universe manifests them.

Affirmations for Changing Thoughts

Affirmations are repeated phases or sentences. They are matrices for casting rather than mantras; they create the pattern that the universe will fill.

Each statement must be carefully crafted. It must be in the present tense, rather than in the future. It must be positive (something good is present) rather than negative (something bad is removed). It must be believable enough that the conscious mind will not reject it.

Affirmations may be about any desired condition and any issue. You can use someone else's affirmation or create your own. Typical affirmations are: "All financial doors are now open to me. All financial channels are now free to me. Divine substance now appropriately manifests for me."[45] "The perfect Life of God now expresses through me, and every part of my body expresses its innate perfection and wholeness."[46]

The magazines of the movement publish monthly collections of affirmations, one for each day. Here is one from *Science of Mind* magazine for March 1992: "I find peace of mind through trusting God. As I place my security in God, right action is established in my life and affairs."

In the same month *Daily Word,* published by the Unity School of Christianity, had this: "The Light of God envelops the earth, and environmental conditions are healed and restored."

Affirmations are not magical. They are tools to change thought; the new belief brings about the change in the world. Emmet Fox said: "An affirmation is often helpful as a memorandum of what you are to believe, but it is the change in your process of thinking from effort to Truth that brings the demonstration — not just the repetition of a phrase."[47]

Creating seems to have the same laws whether you are working for yourself or for another. You make an affirmation about another person, and use it until their experience changes. Such affirmations *must* include respect for their freewill and autonomy. If people are having difficulty bringing about change for themselves, they may hire an experienced practitioner to treat for them.

 ## Visualizations for Creating Belief

While verbal affirmation is the most frequent way of changing belief in the Metaphysical movement, visualization is also very common.

Visualizations to create belief are constructed much like affirmations. They involve seeing the new situation in detail and stepping into it. Visualization might better be called multisensory imagining, in which you continue to visit the desired scene until it manifests.

The Unity School of Christianity long ago created a book that tells people how to visualize by cutting out pictures and making a collage of the wanted result.[48] Many in the New Age have followed suit, producing manuals for visualization. One of the most convincing is David Spangler, who was part of the Findhorn community in Scotland before becoming an independent teacher. His book about the process of manifestation is a step-by-step blueprint for imagining and believing a new world into existence. He also has stories about his own experience — including manifesting a Star-Trek action figure that was very hard to find to complete a friend's collection.[49]

Religious Science practitioner Margaret Stortz says that "all kinds of things fall into place" when praying for others: quarrels and divorces are settled, people reach agreements, jobs are found, obstructions dissolve. "We're all in a state of flow, and a lot of things fall right into line."[50]

Religious Science's founder Ernest Holmes was very clear about the need for real results. "But we should not fool ourselves about any demonstration.... The kind of demonstration we believe in is the kind that can be checked by a physician, if one so desires. If we are treating for the removal of a cancer, we have not made a demonstration until the cancer is gone and the wholeness of the body is evident to everyone. This is not a process of saying 'Peace' when there is no peace."[51]

> Everywhere God will come to meet you,
> everywhere will appear to you,
> at places and times at which you will look not for it,
> in your waking hours and in your sleep,
> when you are journeying by water and by land,
> in the night-time and in the day-time,
> when you are speaking and when you are silent;
> for there is nothing which is not God.
>
> — Hermes Trismegistus[52]

Affirmation and visualization help apply the basic concept that belief creates what is believed. The point in the theme "Belief Creates" is to change consciousness, confident that external conditions will follow.

 Already Perfect Patterns

The second theme in metaphysical prayer is that God is the source of all perfect patterns. In this form of prayer, the Klingbeil family (Christian Science practitioners Bruce

Klingbeil and his children John and Deborah, the creators of Spindrift and the Grayhaven School of Christian Science Nursing) have been my guides. I have quoted from sources other than their beloved Christian Science in an attempt to relate what they are saying to what I already know. But it is their viewpoint I have been trying for ten years to understand, always profiting from the study and always feeling there is more I have not yet understood.

And God saw every thing that he had made, and, behold, it was very good.   — Genesis 1:31 KJV

When we turn our eyes away from the world and toward the Source of All, we see that closer to that Source is the prototype of every good thing. The perfect creation still hovers about its Creator, and all we have to do is look in that direction to see the perfect pattern for every created thing. In this approach, we do not create the image and bring it into existence by our belief. Instead, we look at the prototypical pattern in the Mind of God. And as we contemplate it, it manifests in the world. Those who use this method would phrase it differently. They would say that when we perceive the reality (the perfect pattern), the erroneous mis-patterning is seen through as the illusion it always was.

Find the already-perfect pattern.

This theme says that if we suffer, it is because we have forgotten Reality. Deborah Klingbeil stresses that the intent is not to blame the victim here. Misperception means that we see in dualistic terms and forget that only God's perfection is real. We are like self-disconnected branches, withering and dying without need. The prescription of pattern-directed prayer is to return to our Father's house and, in fact, to discover we've never left it. We will then accept the good that is already our inheritance.

> The blessing of the Lord, it maketh rich,
> and he addeth no sorrow with it.
> — Proverbs 10:22 KJV

Emmet Fox applied this by seeing the presence of God at exactly that place where the problem seemed to be found. By doing so, one will find the qualities of God, such as love: "Scientific Prayer consists in seeing God where the trouble seems to be. When a person seems to be behaving badly, see the Presence of God in him. When a part of the body is sick or damaged, see the Presence of God there. Where there seems to be lack, see the Presence of God and claim Divine Love too, and when you feel the sense of Divine Love your demonstration is made and what you need will come."[53]

The practice that is suggested by the second theme, then, is trust and awareness. The awareness of the presence of God is sufficient to transform the problem that is before the practitioner. It is *all* we need do. If we are looking Godward, we will be illumined by the perfection of God's creation.

A Spiritually Perfect Universe

Christian Scientists, for instance, see the universe as spiritual and perfect. The material universe is a misperception that is simply not accurate. Attending to the spiritual reality is (in their view) paying attention to what is True, and turning away from error. Christian Science founder Mary Baker

Eddy summarized this view in her "Scientific Statement of Being": "There is no life, truth, intelligence, nor substance in matter. All is infinite Mind and its infinite manifestation, for God is All-in-all. Spirit is immortal Truth; matter is mortal error. Spirit is the real and eternal; matter is the unreal and temporal. Spirit is God, and man is His image and likeness. Therefore man is not material; he is spiritual."[54]

> It is utterly simple and it is powerful beyond human conception. It is this very simplicity that causes most people to miss it. It consists in, first believing, and then gradually realizing more and more that God is the only power and that everything we can be aware of is part of His self-expression. That is the whole story — simple but not, of course, easy, because we have lifelong habits of wrong thinking to overcome. — Emmet Fox[55]

This still-radical statement says that Truth includes our spiritual pattern, perfect in every way. Paying attention to those identities has a surprising by-product: conditions in the erroneous, seemingly material universe will improve.

Those patterns are perfect and complete and eternal. They are outside of the change process we call "time." And the eternity that they exist in is beneficent and good. Others in the metaphysical tradition have referred to the perfect pattern as "the angel,"[56] giving an additional poignancy to what Jesus said in Matthew 18:10: "Take heed that ye despise not one of these little ones; for I say unto you, That in heaven their angels do always behold the face of my Father which is in heaven."

Finding Heaven's Pattern

In this form of prayer, we do not create the model. Instead, we seek it "in Heaven." We turn our attention away from what exists in time and space, and turn it toward eternity. In eternity we seek the perfect pattern of the person we are praying for, and we meditate on that pattern.

This pattern is "very good," as it says in Genesis. It is also the Buddha Nature, the "original face before you were born." The New Thought tradition would call it "God expressing in you, as you."

> Universal Mind (Alaya-Vijnana) transcends all individuation and limits. Universal Mind is thoroughly pure in its essential nature, subsisting unchanged and free from faults of impermanence, undisturbed by egoism, unruffled by distinctions, desires and aversions. Universal Mind is like a great ocean, its surface ruffled by waves and surges but its depths remaining forever unmoved.　　—Lankavatara Sutra V

Here is where it gets tricky. The object is *not* to make up a perfect pattern, and *not* to answer the question "What do I wish they were like." The object is to find out what they already are, in eternity.

Deborah Klingbeil emphasizes that "pattern-directed" prayer is not exactly an action. It is more like a receptive act of perception, so it lacks the effortfulness and goal-centeredness of other forms of treatment.

It is common in Christian Science to pray for things that wouldn't seem to have a spiritual pattern. The Klingbeils talk about sitting on the footboard of an old-fashioned truck, and praying for it until it would start.[57] Deborah Klingbeil herself was a nurse at a Christian Science nursing facility, and she recalls that when the elevator broke down the staff would call a repair service. But they would also pray for the elevator. The repairman often arrived to find the elevator working again.

Pattern-directed prayer is excellent for praying for systems, it turns out. Even if you have no idea at all what the best state is for an ecology or an organization, you can look for the spiritual identity anyway, and allow that pattern to manifest in an ideal way. Deborah Klingbeil routinely has the children in her prayer programs praying for rivers, for instance.

> True prayer is not asking God for love; it is learning to love, and to include all mankind in one affection. Prayer is the utilization of the love wherewith He loves us. Prayer begets an awakened desire to be and do good. It makes new and scientific discoveries of God, of His goodness and power. It shows us more clearly than we saw before, what we already have and are; and most of all, it shows us what God is. Advancing in this light, we reflect it; and this light reveals the pure Mind-pictures, in silent prayer, even as photography grasps the solar light to portray the face of pleasant thought. — Mary Baker Eddy, *No and Yes*

In pattern-directed prayer the effect does not come from movement towards a goal, but from the perception of already existing perfection. This is more like sailing with the wind, she said, than motor-boating according to your own desires. The object is to make contact with, to contemplate, that perfect identity. You do not need to do anything except observe it and love it.

> We don't have to always see the true self, just salute it and say hi. If a woman wearing a black veil came to see me I would talk to her and be just as kind as if I could see her face. If she were veiled and did not speak, answer, respond, or move I could not know her but I would know that Someone was in there. Sometimes in prayer you just feel the breathing of the true self, and that faintly. It's a start.
>
> — Deborah Klingbeil

But that should not be taken as an easy task. The perfect identity you're observing is not visible in the ordinary universe. In the ordinary universe you may have clanging disorder. Standing in the midst of that apparent disorder and still turning to and perceiving perfect order requires extreme discipline. And sometimes it still does not happen: you just cannot perceive it.

Working from Divine Principle

When it's impossible to perceive the identity, you're like a pilot trying to find land in the fog. If you can't see it, you have to calculate where it is; then you can fly trustingly in that direction.

Many metaphysical healers may do something similar. Sometimes they cannot directly perceive the spiritual identity of the person they are treating for, so they deduce what it must be like. They work with confidence, because metaphysical practitioners believe that God is principled — in fact, that God is Principle itself. So you might hear someone say something like "Joan is made in the image of God. But God is perfect and whole in every way; so Joan, made in

God's image, must be perfect too. Health is part of perfection, so health must be part of her. Full and complete life is hers now." The reasoning from Principle is not for its own sake — it is to let the practitioner realize the truth about the person being treated.

It is for this reason that Metaphysical healers frequently seem to be rehearsing out loud. They are trying out various aspects of Principle to find the one that will open the way to healing. It must not be just an academic discourse, though. Mary Baker Eddy says: "Instead of scientifically effecting a cure, it starts a petty crossfire over every cripple and invalid, buffeting them with the superficial and cold assertion, 'Nothing ails you.'"[58] Klingbeil adds that sometimes you do say the word before realizing it, but just saying it over and over won't make you realize it. She says: "It's not the saying it but the yearning almost painfully for it — the pearl of great price thing that you would give absolutely everything for — the part of you that protests wholly against a child being in pain — that brings you into the realization. It is just so much not a head thing. The love, the yearning, the 'heart wholly in protest' must be there and should be focused on."

Suddenly the words are not just abstractions. Suddenly they are true and powerful. It is the moment the pilot comes out of the clouds and sees the headlands, and Home.

 Moving Toward the Source

When I think I know what is best, or when I want a certain outcome very strongly, I tend to pray goal-directedly: "Give me that, please!" When I really know that I don't know what is best, I tend to pass the buck "You know what is best and I know I don't. Please, may the Best happen."

And most people have had enough experience with getting what they pray for to know they had better be careful. Dr. Larry Dossey, the great popularizer of prayer in recent decades, wrote a whole book about just that issue, *Be Careful What You Pray For ... You Just Might Get It. . . .*[59] So even when praying for totally specific things, many of us add " ... if it be for the best for me and for all involved." This is not just a formality; it can be very difficult to do. Jesus prayed "thy will be done" as part of the prayer Christians use daily. He also prayed that way the night before he was to be crucified: "My Father, if this cup can't pass away from me, unless I drink it, your will be done."

Come, let us gather all these once more together into a unity and let us say there is a single self-moving power directing all things to mingle as one, that it starts out from the Good, reaches down to the lowliest creation, and returns then in due order through all the stages back to the Good, and thus turns from itself and through itself and upon itself and toward itself in an everlasting circle.

— Hierotheus, *The Hymns of Yearning*[60]

Mostly, though, practitioners have found that following the will of God is an easier path rather than a harder one. Those who ally themselves with wisdom and kindness find that wisdom and kindness smooth the path of service. The two themes, the creativeness of belief and the seeking of spiritual identities, seem to complement one another. Most practitioners work with both approaches.

As God creates by thought, so (in the image of God) do we. Facing toward the manifest universe, say those who emphasize the power of belief, we generate it by thought and are ourselves directors of providence. Facing toward the Source, we return to the prototypes, the perfect Universe as God creates it or, as one might say in East Asia, "Buddha Nature." Each step toward the source brings us towards greater good, because the Source is Good, say those who experience perfect Patterns.

We can treat (the first theme) to allow God's thoughts to come through us (the second theme). If you do this habitually, what seemed to be a self-centered practice of treatment for one specific good can gradually become something more.

The more spiritual treatment you do, the thinner is the fear and resistance laid over the essential, pure, inner light of being.   — Stuart Grayson[61]

LISTENING
FOR GUIDANCE

When a close relative, seemingly suffering from AIDS-related dementia, became homeless, we wondered what we should do. Before he ended up on the street, we visited him and connected him with services that didn't seem to help. Afterwards we found him and tried to get him housing and help. We did the reasonable things.

But each time he declined to follow up on what we and others offered. The social workers who were working with him said he was making choices. We refused to believe it; we were helping (damn it!) and we were not to be thwarted. When I asked inwardly what would be the best way to help, a strange image came to mind. "Let him do what he will," the image seemed to say. "Light a lamp in your heart, and let him come as near the door as he wants to."

Now, I think this is weird and impractical advice. I expected to receive a pointer to a different program, another form of treatment. But I did not have a whole lot else I knew how to do, so I went for the advice; and ever since then there is the sense that he comes near the open round door of my heart and enjoys the radiance. Oh, and I meddle less; and when we go visit him, he is glad to see us.

The Need for Direction

What to do, what to do? That question besets everyone, and it is doubly troubling to a person who is attempting to help others.

When we pray, we have a desperate need for navigation. We are in deep waters when we ask for help for another person because we are always meddling in some way. Our culture has decided very wisely that professional meddlers (doctors, psychologists, lawyers) should have training, licensing, and continuing education to make sure they know what they're doing before we turn them loose. And still it's called "practice."

> Trust in the Lord with all thine heart; and lean not unto thine own understanding.
> In all thy ways acknowledge him, and he shall direct thy paths.
>
> —Proverbs 3:5–6

Prayer is unlicensed and always will be. So how do we avoid doing harm and how do we find the best thing to offer when we pray? Not, perhaps, the perfect thing — but the "locally best" way to help?

We are fortunate that the same Helper who responds to prayer seems willing to help us pray well. But we have to ask, and we have to find ways to listen to the answer.

Doubting our intuitions is not entirely faithless. We know that not every thing that occurs to us is a good idea. We need advice that meets certain standards.

We need the advice to be wise. It should lead to good outcomes for us and for the one we pray for. We're asking that our Advice Giver have better vision than we do. We're asking that it see into our blind spots, so that it knows our failings as well as our strengths. Finally, we ask that the Guide develop us through the practice of prayer. Not only do we want to serve others but (let us admit) we want to get better in the process.

What we do *not* need is explanations. Or, at least, we had better not expect our Guide to give us explanations, because I've never seen one that does. You can get good advice, but apparently those who will help us draw the line at explaining *why* a certain path is good or bad.

 ## Asking a Friend for Advice

All this can make asking for guidance sound like filling out a form in some huge bureaucracy. But asking for Guidance with a capital "G" is just asking a friend for advice, and trying to listen to the answer.

A Public Broadcasting documentary tells of a Cuban-born American, Silvia Morini-Heath, who decided to return to Cuba for a visit.[62] It was a huge move for her because it seemed to be a betrayal of her life-long opposition to Communism. Before she made her final decision, she went to church and asked for advice from her patron, St. Maria Faustina Kowalska. "If it wasn't the right time, then she'd find a way to tell me, okay? But apparently she's telling me it is okay, so let's go."

St. Faustina made no objection, and Silvia went. Was it a wise decision? When Silvia returned to the United States, she became a strong advocate for lifting the embargo against Cuba.

This is what living with intuition is like. You live your daily life, including prayer for others. But threaded through it is a conversation with a wise Advisor.

The Varieties of Guidance

What amazes me most is the variety of ways in which guidance can come when you ask for it.

Rose Rosetree's background is Jewish, Christian, and Hindu. From that broad heritage and her own experience she has named and catalogued some of the ways a person can experience non-ordinary information.[63] Every one of these experiences can also be a channel for guidance.

> In spiritual matters, the best a human being can do is to know his or her whole truth: the most complete and honest set of information, recognized in the ways that are personally most meaningful.
>
> By analogy, if you were praying, would it be your business to compose "the" perfect prayer for everyone? Your job, my job, is to pray our own prayers. Let other people pray theirs. Well, the same goes for subtle perception.
>
> — Rose Rosetree

Rosetree says that *emotional empathy* allows a person to feel some of the feelings of others, nearby or far away, while *physical empathy* allows them to experience the physical sensations of other beings. *Analytic Awareness* is intellectual intuition that allows a person to understand suddenly and accurately. *Holistic knowing* lets people make connections within a system, whether among ideas, people, or other living beings. *Truth knowledge* lets the truth emerge as a thought, often without explanation. *Psychic knowing* is a combination of other perceptive styles, letting information come as feelings or sensations or thoughts.

Guidance to the person who is praying for others can come in any of these forms. The following are experiences of some of the people I pray with:

In a city on a distant continent, the mother of a friend of a friend dies. One might think of all sorts of prayer for this family: ease for the woman who had died, help for the family's grief. But because the person praying trusts his often-experienced *emotional empathy*, he feels that her son needs specific comforting. The son had been caring for his mother, and now seems to feel guilty about his relief at her death. So the prayers for him could acknowledge his feelings and set them in a context of mercy.

A body worker is asked to help a woman receiving chemotherapy in another state. The same *physical empathy* that makes her skillful working with people in person tells her that the distant woman feels a burned desperation. The body worker offers her company and a hammock-like support, and she receives in return a feeling that the woman is able to accept the support and use it to go through her own feelings.

A mathematician looks at a Moebius strip (a loop with a half-twist in it), and *analytic awareness* tells him that Moebius strips could be used to reverse the polarity of waves. Because he also prays for others, he decides that the Moebius strip could be one of the spaces he silently offers to people who need to reverse how they experience things.

An investor in Chicago perceives the fluctuations of the market by *holistic knowing*. His holistic knowing helps him to moderate the market's precipitous drops. "I don't think of what I do as praying, as much as 'keeping company'" he says, "also reassuring and smoothing, and almost always anymore on days when volatility (especially downward volatility) is expected to be high. I try to find market participants as a group and reassure them so that panic doesn't get the better of the whole system."

A woman just learning Therapeutic Touch feels inadequate because she experiences no energy at all. Thoughts keep coming into her mind about the people on whom she is doing Therapeutic Touch. She wants to dismiss them as "just intellectualizing," but their accuracy and relevance suggests that they are *truth knowledge* at work.

Some people see pictures. Some get a feeling. Some really do hear a voice. For some people a word or phrase just appears in their mind. Others perceive aromas — the expression "Something smells funny about this" may have originated with one of them. And modes of perception can change over time. The first guidance I remember came as feelings. Now I often get pictures. Why? I don't know; the change is as mysterious as the advice itself. The point is that all these and other forms of perception can come as guidance in the practice of prayer.

If these perceptions make you uncomfortable because they seem "psychic," consider what Southern Baptist minister Jean Delaney said when she had once again called a friend who was in unspoken need:

She said, "Jean Delaney, every time you call me, something is going on." And this is what she asked me, she said, "Do you have ESP?" And I said, "No, I have HSP." And she said, "HSP?" And I said, "Holy Spirit Power!"

Guidance really is with us all the time. You find your attention is drawn to something. It may be something you've seen many times before, but this time there is a slight eager, positive quality to the way in which you're urged to pay attention. Whatever you're being directed to seems to stand out. It's like the yellow highlighter students use to mark text: "*This* is important."

It's easy to ignore these experiences of "the highlighter" until they're repeated again and again. You're drawn back to a subject repeatedly, and finally you take a class in it and it becomes your life. You keep thinking about one person; you contact them and a deep relationship develops.

But is this guidance, you might wonder, or just attraction, the unconscious, your own temperament at work? We are so resistant to the holiness of the daily life that we demand a pillar of fire before we think we are being guided. It is important to check out purported guidance — more about that later — but it's also important to accept hints when they come.

Talking It Over with God

Tennessee Baptist Jean Delaney takes everything to God in an ongoing conversation. She talks to God all day long. But God does not necessarily speak to her in words. Sometimes God speaks to her in her own "mistakes." She laughed as she told me about missing a turn she had made a thousand times, and ending up at the hospital. Instead of rebuking herself, she said, "OK, Lord. Now I've passed the turn; I'm over here by the hospital. There must be somebody here you want me to see." And there was. An elderly friend was stranded at the hospital entrance with no transportation.

Her dialogues with God are far from formal; they're more like a conversation with a trusted advisor who is not always easy to understand. But they are constantly about what Rev. Delaney should be doing as a servant of God, and as an intercessor.

Sometimes she will be told to pray for people she knows, and sometimes she will have her attention directed to someone she does not know at all: "The name 'Darryl Dawkins' kept coming to mind. And I got up and I went in and I said to my husband, 'Bill, WHO is Darryl Dawkins?' And he said, 'He's a basketball player.' Well, for days, the Lord would have me pray for this man. To this day, I never knew what the results were. To this day, I have never met him. But periodically the Lord would bring this young man's name to mind. And I would pray for him."

I just say, "OK, what are You trying to tell me?"
— Rev. Jean Delaney

I looked up Darryl Dawkins on the Internet, and discovered he played for Detroit in the National Basketball Association. Why Jean Delaney was called to pray for him, I do not know, nor does she. She accepts not knowing what part she is playing. "God," she says, "is the orchestrator."

 Knowing When to Stop

In addition to being guided about what to do, we need to know when to stop — when we are done. Otherwise we will keep on praying in an ever-increasing frenzy.

It seems that *sometimes* there is a sense of answered prayer. A Christian Scientist describes her awareness of the healing of her child while others were sure that her daughter would die: "All this time my mother and the faithful practitioner stood steadfastly by me. My husband and I prayed as we had never prayed before. One day, sitting in the hospital room, I was overcome with a sense of helplessness. The child's condition was not improved under medical treatment. But as I prayed to know that the child was truly in God's care, I was suddenly released from fear and discouragement. Even when one of the doctors said, 'She isn't any worse but don't get your hopes up for she can't possibly live,' I was not impressed or discouraged nor did I doubt it."[64]

Her child recovered. The release from fear and discouragement, a sudden and inexplicable sense of reassurance, can come well before any external sign of the healing. It is important to know that the situation may be healed without such a reassurance. But for those to whom such a sense comes frequently, it can become a guide during prayer.

W. Frederic Keeler is known for the simplicity and austerity of his healing methods. He would ask Spirit if (say) one of his clients was well. If he got a sense of reassurance, which to him was "Yes," he would then ask a second question. He called this second question "the master question"; it was simply to ask if the first response was accurate. He trusted this second answer because he felt that consciousness knew itself. When treating a client, he said, "I will ask: 'Is my chosen decision a right one? Is this conclusion true that John is well?'

"I am now awaiting my answer. I have faith and peace. I await until the thought of assurance comes in.

"Or, if after being still a short time, a peaceful time... should no assurance come into my consciousness, then I know that I was not right and that I have been corrected."[65]

 Testing the Guidance

So how do we avoid being stone crazy when we pay attention to our intuition, to our guidance? There are, I think, short-term tests and long-term tests.

The long-term test is fairly simple — what happens if you follow the guidance? With any intuitive method or form of guidance, you should of course try it out on things that do not have life-or-death importance. Try it out on the small stuff first.

Accept that you are the responsible party. You might ask, "How can I be the responsible party if I am getting direct guidance from God?" Let me say it directly: Some awful people have made the same claim.

Our job is to do what Jesus suggested, and see what the fruits of the advice may be. Do we end up better? Do those we are praying for end up better? Or do we become a little weirder, a little crabbed, with a complicated view of the world necessary to explain how screwy our life is?

When the guidance is weird, be suspicious of it. If it tells you to do something you think is wrong, it is probably worth ignoring or at least checking many times. It's perfectly all right to say to your inner guide, "I'm sorry, you said *what?*" Treat it the same way as you would treat a human advisor who told you to do something dubious.

I do not recommend that you follow guidance that is truly fearful for you. It is my experience that with inner guidance the path is easy, and not a sacrifice, testing ground, or a challenge.   —Lee Coit[66]

The short-term test is the feeling quality the intuition has. Baptist Rev. Delaney, Franciscan nun Sister Colette, and *Course in Miracles* teacher Lee Coit all emphasize that one quality associated with bad advice is *fear.* The presence of reassurance and the absence of fear are marks of good advice.

We all have fearful inner voices and feelings. They are attempting to protect us, no doubt, guarding us from the fearful events of our own lives or of our parents' lives or of our culture's lives. But real guidance seems to come from a place where fear does not live. Sister Colette said: "The feeling that is associated with the Devil is fear. He likes to appear as an angel of light, but that doesn't last."

Rev. Delaney said that when fear comes to her, she recalls 2 Timothy 1:7. "For God hath not given us the spirit of fear; but of power, and of love, and of a sound mind."

If the advice is from a good, kind, wise God, that good kindness and wisdom will almost always be obvious in what happens afterwards. I only say "almost" because some things happen out of our sight, and we never know the outcome. In most cases we will eventually find out what the story is.

Avoid fearful advice, but you will sometimes get *odd* advice. After some experience with intuition you come to trust even these peculiar counsels.

Nancy and I were looking for an Australian Shepherd to replace our lamented dog Abigail. We had driven a hundred miles to the Salinas Valley to see a puppy. He was a perfectly satisfactory dog, good looking and vigorous, but my intuition said "No." Whenever I get a weird answer from my intuition, I ask again (sometimes several times), and I did. The same answer. We drove home in a glacial silence.

A bit later we heard about a puppy in the Sierra foothills, again a long trip, and we went looking. We found the small brown puppy and she captured us at first glance. We tried to maintain a little sales resistance, and failed. She came home with us that night and delights us still, a perfect companion dog. Oh, and the same intuition said "Yes" to her.

Was the intuition directing us to wait so we could find an even better dog? I think so; I think the "fruits" of following that strange intuitive message were very good. But it is important to check your intuition frequently. It's not that the advice is necessarily bad, but our hearing can get a little off. We need to constantly recalibrate our instrument, just as we would with any fine tool.

When we do check our intuition by watching its results, however, we end up with a Guide who will lead us through difficult times when we ourselves cannot see. And guidance will come — sometimes odd, usually commonsensical, and very reliable.

 ## Listening to Inner Guidance

Lee Coit wrote *Listening* from his own experience with following guidance. He began as a skeptic. But his life was in tatters, and he was willing to try anything for a while to find out "if life makes sense." Part of his experiment was to travel to Europe and to follow his inner guidance in everything he did.

TEN SUGGESTIONS
FOR BETTER LISTENING

We need to be still.
Have no investment in the answer to the question.
Listen with assurance.
God's voice is everywhere.
Accept the answer.
Be patient.
There is only One Voice.
If in doubt, "Keep Listening."
Listen for Reassurance
Daily devotion.

— Lee Coit

He came to distinguish two inner voices. One was fearful and hurried, and at first that was the louder voice. But if he declined to listen to that fearful voice, he could hear another voice that was peaceful and fearless and loving. By constantly listening to that second voice, he came to hear it first and then almost exclusively. And that unafraid voice was his inner guidance.

At the Swedish border, for instance, there was a large and unruly crowd trying to get through customs. Other tourists were pushing and complaining. Coit's intuition told him to love everyone and that all would be taken care of. He went outside and took a few pictures, and when he returned he found himself quickly and smoothly getting through. At every step of his trip he was guided to helpful and friendly people, good accommodations, and even gasoline during a fuel shortage.[67]

If you seek guidance more than anything else, you're probably making a good choice. Solomon did, and God was pleased and gave him everything else he asked for,[68] including the admiration of the Queen of Sheba.[69] Asking for guidance, checking the guidance against common sense, and gradually coming to rely on it may lead you to interesting places. Most of those places seem kindly. That kindness is the same, I believe, as that which motivates us to pray for others in the first place.

DISCOVERING MEANING, HEALING, AND SOUL HELP

"Leva," a patient on whom I was working with Northern California bodyworker Bobbie Jurgenson, had a serious and painful condition. As we worked, though, a grief attached to anger kept coming through. Bobbie was doing all the bodywork, so I was available to follow the feelings.

Leva said that in the first few months of her mother's pregnancy her mother had been told that she was carrying not a child but a tumor. Leva had been in her mother's womb for months before she was recognized. The un-recognition, the feeling of not being seen, had persisted through her whole life.

Not to see Leva is a crime: she is a glowing coal of life. So while Bobbie worked on her body, I just followed Leva back to before even the moment of her conception, and came forward with her. Every so often we would stop in time, and I would simply *see* her. Forward we came through birth, childhood, girlhood, and young-womanhood to the present. As we arrived at "now," Leva was indeed here. Her native fire and presence shown out of her eyes.

Later that afternoon Leva was trying to get the attention of a rowdy group of people. In the past she would not have succeeded. This time she stuck her fingers in her mouth and with a howling whistle, commanded their attention. Leva was seen.

The Work of Modern Shamans

We know very little about shamanism in its ancient forms. There are stories of people who were called to heal, to divine the future, and to battle for their tribes in the spirit lands. They learned to travel out of body to other worlds. They talked to beings that most people could not communicate with. They brought prosperity and health to their tribes by "singing down power." They were subject to strange dreams and visions. Their bodies glowed with heat when they worked. They retrieved lost souls. They escorted the dead to the next world.

Shamanism might seem to be a set of fossilized footprints by a long-dead stream. Yet some of the prints are fresh.

You might meet someone who wears the label "shaman" who really is one, and you may meet people doing shaman's work but without the title. It might be a man or a woman from an indigenous people who have preserved an unbroken tradition of shamanic work. An old woman may have initiated her in the forest; an old man may have taught him to drum in a snow-bound hut.

We all come from ancient peoples, of course, and if you were born in this universe you are indigenous. Sometimes now the initiators are former academics who decided they would rather *do* shamanism than theorize about it.

Michael Harner is an American anthropologist who studied shamans in the Amazon.[70] Then he studied shamanism. Then he practiced shamanism, and now for several decades he has taught it to others.[71]

One time, as I lay asleep, a dream came to me — I heard singing up in the sky. Because I was little, because I didn't realize what it was, I didn't pay (conscious) attention to it — I just (passively) listened when that man was singing up above. Still he made it known to me — it was as if it entered deep into my chest, as if the song itself were singing in my voice box. Then it seemed as if I could see the man, as if I could just make him out.

After I awoke from sleep, that song was singing itself inside me all day long. Even though I didn't want to sing, still the song was singing in my voice box. Then I myself tried, tried to sing, and amazingly the song turned out to be beautiful. I have remembered it ever since.

—Essie Parrish, Pomo Indian Shaman[72]

Michael and Sandra Harner teach basic shamanism to large and happy crowds of students. Their teaching has found echoes in the souls of many who never thought of themselves as members of a "shamanic people," and I have been grateful to find such initiation within my own culture.

The city traffic roared on Mission Street four floors below as the shaman looked out the window and found the moon. I had come to the California Institute of Integral Studies in San Francisco to interview Antonio Ramirez, a shaman born in Mexico and now practicing in the United States. He was a Marxist and a thoroughly modern man until paranormal experiences drew him to Spirit. He learned first from Jose Silva of Silva Mind Control and then from Michael Harner before he went to traditional sources in the Amazon and among California Indians.

At the end of the interview, I asked him to do his work for me. He first found the moon, then stood behind me as I was sitting in a chair, and put his hands on my shoulders. Then he began to tremble, with about the same frequency as a hand-trembler's hand vibrations,[73] and put his hands on the back of my head. I could feel something flowing down inside my head, down into my torso. He continued to move his hands and question me about my experience until at one point he leaned over and blew into the top of my head. I have no idea what he was blowing in or out. My vision cleared with a snap, the table in front of me coming abruptly into focus. I suddenly felt very, very present.

After touching my body on the shoulders, arms, head, and stomach and apparently channeling power into it for a while, Ramirez began to sing a melody with words that sounded very much like American Indian songs. He said of it later, "The sound was carrying a motion that was, that goes always ahead — kind of the future. So I saw these kind of tentacles going into the future."

While he was singing the song, and before he had told me about what his experience was, I too had had a vision of something reaching out and branching, like a silvery river rising and spreading down channels.

 ## The Children of Abraham

Shamanic work is also found within Abrahamic traditions. The ascents into heaven, the prophesying, the Night-Journey of Muhammad to Jerusalem, and the long carriage ride that took Chassidic Judaism's founder, the Baal Shem Tov, hundreds of miles in one night — all of these would seem shamanic to people from cultures in Siberia or Malaya.

They demonstrate that this family of blessing styles is available within Judaism, Christianity, and Islam. But what does that mean in practice?

The Sorcerers and Curers have their Language as well, but it is different from mine. They ask favors from Chicon Nindó. I ask them from God the Christ, from St. Peter, from Magdalene and Guadalupe. — María Sabina, Mazatec Shaman[74]

The Kabbalah, with its ladder that runs between heaven and earth and its practices of changing consciousness, preserves within Judaism the shamanic custom of singing down power. Shneor Stern is a Chassidic rabbi, a member of the Lubavitcher community. He talked to me at the San Francisco Lubavitcher community's center on the edge of Chinatown in San Francisco. Rabbi Stern said, "In the Kabbalah, it says that prayer and song are really one and the same...."

Stern says that the Kabbalah predicts that musicians will enter into a three-dimensional psychedelic realm of music, which is like a living cathedral of music. The song itself, the playing of the song, takes on another dimension, as if it's an entire world that you can see, hear, smell, taste, and feel. "There will be a transcendence into a state of awakeness, into a state of Divine awakening, and a major source of prophetic vision and insight and information will be music."

Rabbi Stern is himself a singer, and at my request he sang both a traditional song and one of his own composition in a pure voice, without vibrato, filled with longing and nostalgia for God. It was not like a hymn or a chant. It was too personal, like a love-song or a keen.

Sound is a connector. The first space it resonates in is the body. Sound is vibration that connects the body (and

95

the singer) to the larger physical space.[75] Tradition insists that it also connects with the world of spirit and power. The songs have an effect on the space in which they are sung, Stern said; and the spaces come to resonate with the consciousness of the songs sung in them. "Once we realize the eternity of now, then we can realize — and this is what we're doing — we're climbing a ladder, it's in a sense a meditative ladder, as if we were going up to the higher resources and drawing down light and life energy, and then bringing this creational energy into the world to heal and enlighten and transform the world."

Whither shall I go from thy spirit? or whither shall I flee from
    thy presence?
If I ascend up into heaven, thou *art* there: if I make my bed
    in hell, behold, thou *art there.*
If I take the wings of the morning, *and* dwell in the uttermost
    parts of the sea;
Even there shall thy hand lead me, and thy right hand shall
    hold me.   —Psalm 139:7–10 KJV

As I looked at these words from my interview with Rabbi Stern, I noticed how perfectly they described my experience with the shaman Antonio Ramirez.

Our daily world is meaning-deprived. It is as if there is not enough meaning to fill all the events of our universe. But shamanic experiences are just the opposite: they are dense with meaningfulness.

 ## The Use of Animal Power

Harner's basic class teaches you how to visit the Lower World to find a power animal for another person. While one or more people drum, the traveler lies down beside the person for whom they are undertaking the journey and enters the world undergirding this one — not a hell-world, but a world of conscious plants and animals. They continue to search until an animal shows itself to them four times. They bring that animal back and, rising from their trance, blow it into the heart and head of the client. Then they tell the recipient the animal they have found. People who have had that experience have felt a sudden increase in meaningfulness and relationship with the natural world.

Sometimes the animals come before the experience. A friend of mine took one shamanism workshop years ago — after having decided not to — because a pelican seemed to appear in her office. She took the class, and still greets pelicans with "Hello, buddy!" each time she sees one flying along the coast.

It is important to realize that the experience that the shaman and perhaps the client have had is *shamanic* and not *objective*. Shamanic teacher and author Sandra Ingermann says, "Because the information in journeys often comes metaphorically, I am careful not to report my experiences as literal, although they sometimes are."[76]

It may be exactly and literally true about the physical world, or it may be a metaphor for something obvious, or it may be almost uninterpretable. But meditation on it will bring meaning. Just as energy work can be a blessing to the touch-deprived, so by shamanic journeys you can help those you pray for with the sense of meaninglessness and *anomie.* I don't know how it works, but I have experienced it often enough to know it is reliable. It is as if the shaman's journey leads to the land from which significance itself comes and permits the visitor to bring it back for others.

Many people try to apply ordinary-reality tests to shamanic experience, not knowing that it usually begins quite subtly and builds strength as it is attended to.

I worked with a man in one of the Harners' classes who "couldn't see anything." The exercise involved journeying while the Harners beat on big, flat drums. It was a deeply entrancing rhythm, and most people had very vivid imagery of traveling to strange, far places. When the drumming ended, we were invited to sit up and trade stories with our partners. "I'll go first," he said. "It'll be quick. Nothing happened for me."

I found it odd that nothing at all happened in such a hypnotic environment. So I asked him what he *had* experienced. "Darkness," he said. "All I saw was darkness."

"Really?" I asked. "What was it like?"

"Dark," he said.

"Was there anything in the darkness?"

"No," he said, " . . . except the eyes."

Then for a half hour he told about the eyes he had seen in the darkness, the owls they belonged to, and the nocturnal world that he had visited on the journey.

As in keeping company and receiving guidance, the would-be shamanic traveler must restrain self-doubt. Critical thinking is appropriate and necessary, but in the initial stages it can suppress the very subtle beginnings of the experience.

 Recovering the Spirit

Sometimes we say a person is "dispirited," or that they have "lost heart" or "gone away." Shamanic cultures would say that these are literal diagnoses. Moments of shock can make fragments of the soul depart the body.

Some of the Harners' students have revived the practice of soul retrieval. It's a matter of going and finding the part of a person that vanished during stress, and returning it to them. Of all the forms of shamanic blessing, this may be the most intense — an other-world journey that results in the client becoming more present in this world.

> When a human has "lost his soul," the shaman works himself into ecstasy by means of a special technique; while he remains in that state, his soul travels to the world of spirits. Shamans contend to be able, for instance, to track down the lost soul in the underworld in the same way as a hunter tracks down game in the physical world.... Once they have recaptured the lost soul, they bring it back and restore it to the deprived body, thus achieving the cure.
>
> — G. V. Ksenofontov[77]

Sandra Ingerman describes the quest to find lost portions of a person's soul.[78] It begins with setting the intention. The shaman asks power animals to attend and help, and continues with a journey like that described in the previous section. It is not difficult to find these fragments, says Ingerman, and they come back willingly to be reunited in the person's body.

The experience is much like working with subpersonalities in psychosynthesis[79] or some kinds of inner-child work. It is the shaman rather than the client who does the searching and the reuniting, says Ingerman, as we did when working with Leva.

The most common of the lost souls (in my experience) are not frightened and helpless but strong and beautiful. People don't seem to know their strengths. They sometimes think of themselves as hurt and in need of healing, when what they need is to express their own excellences. It's possible to look into a person and see their virtues that have not yet become real to them. If you can lure them out of the cave where they have hidden, you can hold up a mirror and they will see their own splendor.[80]

It is not at all a matter of suggestion. Rather you journey into their essence to find the superb qualities that are already there. This is why shamans do not seek accusing animals or even healing animals, but power animals. This form of blessing is shamanic because shamans retrieve power. The best power is that which lives in people's own natures, their own portion of Beauty.

 ## The Shamanic Art of Communication

Part of the shaman's skill is the ability to talk to beings who do not seem to have speech. Usually that is taken to mean talking with birds and the animals in the forest, and it is true that sometimes a raven speaking outside the window may bring messages from a distant shaman.

There are shamans who can speak with the earth and feel what is well or ill with the land. This is one of the most important aspects of Feng Shui when it is practiced by intuition rather than by rote — first listening to a place and then accommodating its needs.

Communication is not always with separate beings. Holly Reed in San Francisco, for instance, is a body-talker, one of those who communicate with living tissue. Having been raised to believe that silence is the pathway to healing, I would not have realized her power had I not been at a retreat with her fifty miles from the nearest town. In the rainy dark of a California spring night, I wrenched my knee so badly that I dislocated my fibula, the smaller bone in my lower leg. It was the sort of injury that would call for a hospital trip, and then weeks of recovery.

She had me sit on the couch. Her talk was not directed any more at me, but at my leg. She talked to the bones, she spoke to the ligaments, she asked them how they felt. She kept up a quiet stream of conversation with the knee and the bones around it, gently touching them but never pushing them in any way.

As she spoke, the bones and muscles seemed to relax, the tendons came out of shock. Then with a slight internal sigh — a kind of relaxation of guardedness and a letting go — the bone slid back into place. She kept talking, and the injury seemed to reverse itself. It took maybe twenty minutes of conversation, and the damage was almost completely healed. It felt as if the injury had happened a month before, and had recovered well.

At another event I had managed to scald myself seriously and was looking forward to a long recuperation with a damaged right hand. Again she talked to the tissue, this time specifically to the burned cells. Again she spoke without coercing them in any way. The cells relaxed, and the heat left them. It had felt as if the cells had concluded that they were dead from the burn, but as she spoke, they reconsidered. They stopped the orderly process of dying that cells know so well and began to live again. They cooled. Feeling came back into them. In the end after the healing flow of her speech there was only a slight reddening and a little roughness in the skin.

 Helpers for the Dead

In traditional societies, shamans are called to help the dead find their way between the worlds. Sometimes their work is to find a soul that has gone too early, and to bring it back. In this role they are sometimes successful, and the person who revives may have a near-death experience to narrate.

Equally often it is their job to help a confused and disoriented spirit move from the physical world to their next life. If someone dies suddenly and without expecting to, they may simply not know that they are dead. They wander in a physical world with which they can no longer interact, haunting the living until someone helps them move into the wider freedom that spiritual being can confer. Spiritualists often have "rescue circles," whose task it is to assist such earthbound souls.

Ambrose and Olga Worrall were healers for their whole lives. They perceived psychically, traveled outside their bodies and healed both by touch and at a distance. If they had been born in an archaic culture, they would have been called shamans. Having been born in Scotland and America, they were Methodists who did much of their work in Methodist churches in Baltimore, in healing clinics created with the churches' pastors.[81]

In prayer, neither time nor space presents formidable barriers.

—Ambrose Worrall[82]

Both Olga and Ambrose Worrall helped people "make the transition." Ambrose was a supervisor at an aircraft plant — making enough money so that he and Olga never charged for their healing work — when his men came back from an evening meal. Biographer Cerutti tells the story:

"As the men returned, Ambrose looked up and noticed that something about Jack seemed strange. He sat at his workbench but he looked obviously bewildered. When he talked to somebody near him, there was no response. When he tried to pick up a tool, he couldn't because his hand went through it. Suddenly Ambrose realized that Jack was not Jack as he usually was; he was in spirit. But why? He had been well and alive only one hour before!

"Ambrose called Jack telepathically to come to him because he knew that no one else in the room could see Jack. The poor man came near, half in tears, and Ambrose tried to find out what had happened. It was immediately apparent that Jack didn't know; that he was terribly disturbed at being ignored by his co-workers; and that he sensed that something was wrong but couldn't understand what.

"When Ambrose attempted to explain to Jack that in the interval between leaving and returning to work something had ended his life, Jack protested wildly. It was ridiculous, it couldn't be! When Ambrose realized that he himself was not getting through to Jack or fully convincing him of the fact of his death, Ambrose asked the help of specific spirit entities with whom he had previously worked, to take Jack in hand and lead him away.

"Then Ambrose turned to the men who were busy with their jobs. He told them that Jack had been fatally injured and he sent one of them out to find out what had happened. In just a few minutes, the verification was brought back; Jack had been hurrying to the plant after having had a quick meal at home. He had been crossing the railroad tracks, somehow unaware of an oncoming train which unfortunately hit him and killed him instantly."[83]

Only a few people have a calling to work with spirits, and the criterion is simple: If you can perceive them in some way, it may be that you should learn to help them. But everyone can learn a simple blessing for spirits that invites beings that are "farther along" to come and help them. There is a mantra in Buddhism (OM AMI DEWA HRIH) that means "Om. Limitless Light. Compassion." It is an invitation for peace and kindness to come help both the embodied and the unembodied. I think it would work for anyone, without giving offense.

 ## Unlabeled Shamans

In India the practice of austerity is called *tapas*. Asceticism, in the Hindu understanding, gives the practitioner more and more power, eventually enough power to challenge even the Gods.[84]

The word *tapas* actually means "heat." In Tibet there is a practice called *tummo* ("courageous woman" in Tibetan) in which the practitioner learns to develop internal "fire" until they can dry wet sheets on their naked body in the icy midwinter.[85] All of these heat exercises seem to come from a still older tradition of shamanic fire.

Some years ago I met a craftswoman who radiated this heat. She has worked for years in the trades, since well before most women did heavy craft-work. Hidden under the T-shirts and down jackets is a years-old practice of praying for others. She doesn't talk a lot about her practice, and she usually does it alone. She knew of my interest, however, and perhaps for that reason let me be around her while she was practicing.

When she does energy work on people, they can feel intense warmth from her hands. Even among energy workers the degree of heat is remarkable. It is like diathermy, penetrating and also relaxing. It happens whenever she is working for others.

One day I was around her when she was doing her "distant work" for people far away. It took a moment to discover what I was noticing. It felt as if she was radiating heat. It was not, of course, physical heat; it was that same mysterious energy discussed in the chapter on energy work. But she was the source, and it was only present while she practiced. From five feet away it seemed as if I were standing near a Franklin stove in midwinter.

Among the unlabeled shamans are some people who do not think of themselves as such, and in fact would deny it.

I know a very caring skeptic who would go out of her way to give a person a ride. It was on such a trip that we discussed her non-experiences with prayer and blessing. It was, she said, like a deafness in her. She just did not experience any of the energies or entities that seemed real to me. "We must be in bodies for a reason," she said. "Bodies are a gift and opportunity to be practical, and 'going off' is a way of ignoring and not honoring them."

What she said was certainly understandable for me; I have known many people who feel the same way. But then we passed a raccoon who had been killed on the highway and was lying by the side of the road. I paused for a moment to wish the raccoon well in his journey. And so did she. "Blue light," she said. "I look to see if there is any blue light stuck or trying to rise. If there is, I encourage it to spiral up out of the body."

Then she went on explaining how she did not perceive any of the stuff we had been talking about.

SACRIFICING FOR OTHERS

Sacrifice. Can there be in all of religion an older, fiercer word? We know it in modern usage as the practice of giving up something up for another, or for a higher purpose. "He sacrificed himself for his family." "Education requires sacrifices, and she made them." Behind those modern uses of the word swim older and often bloodier meanings: It used to be that beings were killed to make an offering to gods.

But the evolution of religion has by no means removed sacrifice from prayer.

At least three forms of sacrifice are part of praying for others: offering suffering and austerities; offering good deeds (and also the merits received from them); and offering energy in the form of desire and delight.

 Offering Up Suffering

In all of the world's large religions, there has been a personalization of sacrifice in the last two thousand years. Sacrifices that used to be imposed on animals have been taken inside of the sacrificer, so that what is offered comes from the one who makes the offering, rather than from another being. Buddhism, wherever it has gone, has discouraged blood sacrifice and forbidden it entirely within its own temples. Christianity treats the sacrifice of Jesus as the last blood sacrifice.

Many of the older religions that once practiced blood offerings have also relinquished them. Although Judaism once again is in control of Jerusalem, the practice of animal sacrifice has not been resumed. And when Fritz Staal and Robert Gardner attempted to recreate a Vedic Hindu ritual in India for their film *Altar of Fire*, the Indian villagers objected successfully to the death of real animals in the sacrifice. At the moment when the Brahman priest pours clarified butter into the fire, a smell of barbecue arises, and the memory comes of what the sacrifice once was. But it is only a memory.

> While in college, I read about a vision St. Jerome had of the Child Jesus. Memory fails, I must paraphrase: Jesus asked Jerome why he hadn't given Him everything. Jerome was mystified. "Lord," he protested, "I have devoted my life to your service. I have given you all my works, all my love, all my praise, everything." "No," Jesus replied, "You haven't given me your sins." Give it over, offer it up.
>
> — Broderick Barker[86]

What does remain is the offering of personal austerity and suffering. Why does it have such power? How is God compelled by our own suffering to accept the prayers we make for another? It has never been clear, yet it is a tradition that goes back before the beginnings of monotheism.

Lurking behind the apparent submission to God is another idea: That austerity creates power for the one who practices the austerities. The word "asceticism" comes from a Greek word meaning the training of an athlete. In India, the *tapas* that is translated as "austerities" (or "heat") gives so much power that one can battle with and eventually over-come the gods. In offering suffering and austerity, one is also creating power.

I was taught, at St. Joachim's Catholic School in Costa Mesa, California, by nuns of great kindness. Sister Pius was the principal, and she hid in her habit pieces of candy which she would produce for the children at recess. Fifty children might be in a classroom. For all the crowding, we learned reading, writing, and prayer.

We also learned that we lived inside an economy of sac-rifice. In every classroom there was a crucifix, an image of a man nailed to a cross of wood and left to die in the noonday sun. Crucifixion was the form of execution the Roman Empire used for non-citizens, while Roman citizens (like Paul the Apostle) received the comparatively painless beheading. Crucifixion was slow and awful suffering. We learned at St. Joachim's that God had chosen to come into the world and take on that suffering so that all the sin-debt in the world would be paid at once. Nothing could compel an infinite Being to do this: Out of love he had sacrificed himself.

In the church at the school, at least once a day, the sacri-fice was repeated in the Mass. In Catholic doctrine the Mass is not a commemoration of the Passover supper in Jerusa-lem and the death of Jesus on Calvary. The Mass *is* those events themselves, made present in the present moment. We in our crinkly parochial-school uniforms went into the church; and from the time we were very young, we ate the Body of the God who had voluntarily died in pain that we might live forever in Heaven. In such an atmosphere we learned that we could join in the sacrifice. We too could offer our lives and our pains, even small ones, and join the suffering God in redeeming the world. So we gave up our favorite foods for Lent, prayed long rosaries that we did not wish to pray, and offered up our sufferings.

Pray that my sacrifice and yours be made acceptable....
— The Roman Catholic Mass[87]

There is a whole literature about how sacrifice can be neurotic, which has masked the equal possibility that it can be very holy. I found a remarkable essay about suffering written by Charles Delhez, S.J., posted on the web site of the Congregation of the Sacred Heart.[88] He warns against the desire for suffering for its own sake: " . . . we must not forget Christ's prayer in the garden of Gethsemane: 'Abba, Father, everything is possible for you. Take this cup away from me!' However he added (how long did it take him to pronounce this second phrase?): 'But let it be as you, not I, would have it' (Mk 14:36), the will not that Christ should suffer, but that he accomplish his mission of love. . . . In fact there is an implicit or missing link in this spiritual attitude of offering. What is agreeable to God is in fact the love which can find its place in the very heart of suffering."

"Offering Up" is the secret of sacrificial prayer for others. We take an experience that is painful or difficult, whether imposed on us or chosen voluntarily, and we treat it as a sacrifice rather than as an oppression. The first consequence is peace of mind. As columnist Mary Costello said: "But even back when I was totally resistant to the idea of giving anything up, the healthier part of me knew that 'Offer it up' helped me clear out some of the rubbish that cluttered my mind, the mental flotsam and jetsam that seemed to get in the way of my becoming the whole / holy spiritual person

I was meant to be. Today, when I can get past that child-ish, immature resistance to not satisfying my every whim, 'Offer it up' can lead me to a place of total contentment and peace — the 'still waters' of the psalmist."[89]

The most common application of these austerities is the help of others. In the Catholic practice of The Way of the Cross, one prays before fourteen stations that represent events during Christ's last day. When one has completed the small pilgrimage, promises my old Catholic missal, there is granted a plenary indulgence: a soul can leave Purgatory, free to rise to heaven.[90]

Arlette, at seventeen, contracted leukemia at a time when it was an incurable disease. In the midst of this trial, which she knew was mortal, she discovered God who loved her and was waiting for her. She started spreading joy throughout the hospital wards. She approached those who were suffering and restored their taste for life. Her life took on meaning when death had already taken her by the hand.

However one day she was unable to stop herself from screaming with pain. This was a blow to her image of pluckiness. She was not proud of herself when she took stock of the day during her evening prayers: "Well! I certainly am no saint! And if — this time — I didn't know how to suffer 'in silence,' I'll simply offer you my screams!" Instead of moping and overanalyzing her humiliation she presented herself to God and offered herself as she was: not as a heroine, a champion of stoical suffering, but as a girl who had "broken down."

— J'offrirai d'avoir gueulé, letters and notes
by Arlette, presented by Joseph Brosseau, Ed.
Ouvrières, 1968, p. 133.[91]

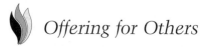 *Offering for Others*

In Judaism you often hear the expression, "It's a mitzveh." *Mitzvah* literally means "commandment" in Hebrew, but the Yiddish word *mitzveh* has taken on a special meaning: an act of charity with merit. It's a word used to convince oneself to do a good deed. Usually one goes for it, and the good deed is done.

I wonder how many times in the day someone does a kindness for someone else: a door is held open, a bus waits for a running patron, a dollar is given to someone homeless, a cruel true word is not said. Often the kindnesses are unrecorded by anyone: they are simply done and forgotten by the doer, a tiny sacrifice. They are not abstract — these are very concrete acts, wise, even canny, sometimes hugely risky. Peter Ferber, a member of a Buddhist mailing list to which I belong, wrote that the secret lies in a balance. If you find only yourself real, you can fall into self-absorption. If you find only the situation real you can be overwhelmed. Peter said: "I've decided that true compassion lies in the details: making myself and the reality of a particular situation real allows for compassion...." He then told the story of "...a Vietnamese colleague who escaped his native land on a crowded boat during the Vietnam war. They were out at sea for many weeks: cold, hungry, but hopeful. They were picked up at one point by a Thai general who did a peculiar thing. The general ordered the boat taken far out to sea, and then he ordered his men to point their guns down at the water and completely discharge their weapons into it. After having performed this command, the general told the assembled boat people that he had been ordered to shoot them. Had the general's men returned to base with loaded rifles, his superiors would know that the order had not been carried out."

These worldly-wise, concrete acts of service to other beings are some of the best things we do in our lives. It is impossible to imagine a world persisting in which no one does such kindnesses. "Society is kindness," said the Dalai Lama.

 Giving Away the Merit

The sense of most religions is that there is an accounting in which all good deeds are recorded and given their due. This credit is called "merit," and there is often a belief that the merit will bring about good things for the person who has done the good deed. It is particularly moving that many people not only do the deed, they also give away the credit. In Islam, for instance, the most common prayer for the dead is to give them the merit of prayers said or of good deeds done. When I interviewed the Shi'ite Imam Mehdi Khorasani, he said: "...to bless the soul or a person's being, to bless him we recite some Quran and intend that the good things of recitation of Quran be given as a gift to that soul of the person who passed away or the person who is alive. We recite a piece of Quran — a *sura*, a chapter of Quran — and offer the good things of it to that person, alive or dead. That is one way. But another way is that we say two units of prayer — which is the similar prayer that daily we pray but extra — we pray two units or four units of prayer and offer the blessing of that prayer, to his soul and to his personality.

"Sometime we say for his pleasures we give food to the poor, we give money to needy persons, that the blessing of that action goes for that person who is passed away or that person who is alive and sick, we want to make him recover,

DEDICATION OF MERIT

By this merit, may all attain Omniscience.
May the enemy, wrong doing, be defeated,
From the stormy waves of old age, sickness and death.
May all beings be liberated.

At this very moment, for the peoples and nations of the
    earth
May not even the names disease, famine, war, and suffering
    be heard;
But rather may their moral conduct, merit, wealth, and
    prosperity increase
And may supreme good fortune and well being always arise
    for them.

Just as the hero Manjusri gained Omniscience
And Samantrabhadra exactly the same,
I dedicate this merit entirely (to the welfare of all)
So that I may train myself to follow Them.[92]

we feed people, and we give help to others that he would recover earlier."

In Mahayana Buddhism, there is a customary ending to any devotional or ceremonial act. One acknowledges that the deed creates merit, that all acts have consequences, and that we live within that web of consequences. In Theravada Buddhism, to some extent, and overwhelmingly in the Mahayana, there is a belief that we can also influence the karma of others with our good deeds. Hence, there too the practice has arisen of giving merit away. As Sam Webster says, "At the end of this practice, as with all practices, we dedicate the benefit of our actions towards the eventual enlightenment of everything that can be enlightened. By doing so it takes the 'merit,' the good energy we have raised and the beneficial karma we have produced and stores it where it will do the most good. By getting it out of our hands we cannot harm it through negative thoughts, words or actions and it continues to benefit us completely because we are among the people we have dedicated the merit of our actions to."[93]

When someone has harmed us, we know in our bones and our teeth that we have a right to strike back.

Christianity has talked about forgiveness for so long that we have perhaps become numb to just what we're offering when we forgive someone — we are sacrificing our *right* to make them suffer as we have suffered.

> A prayer found on a pious Jew in the camp of Treblinka expresses forgiveness in a shattering way: "Lord, when you return in glory, don't only remember the men and women of good will. Remember also the men and women of evil will. But do not remember their cruelty, their ill-treatment, their violence. Remember the fruit we culled because of what they did to us. Remember the patience of some people, the courage of others, the good companionship, the humility, the nobility of soul, the faithfulness they awakened in us. And, Lord, make the fruits we have culled be their redemption one day."[94]

It is a good thing, I think, to forgive. But it should never be routine. Each act of forgiveness is an individual sacrifice, sometimes a great one, of our right to retaliate.

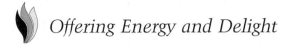 *Offering Energy and Delight*

If we offer our pain and our service, we are within the world of customary religion. Beyond them, sometimes suspect, is the offering of pleasure and beauty. Religions around the world have perceived that there is an energy present in delight, and that the same energy is part of the delight of Creation mentioned in Genesis 1:31: "God saw all that He had made, and behold, it was very good."

Max Freedom Long was an eccentric who went to Hawaii and did not, according to his own accounts, find the living magical tradition of Huna. The secret eluded him in Hawaii; though he heard many stories he was not able to find someone to initiate him. It was not until he returned to the mainland and studied the Hawaiian language that he found what he believed to be the secret of the pre-missionary Hawaiian magical and religious practice.

His language studies suggested to him that the Hawaiian priests (the *kahunas*) had believed in a three-part being. One part was the unconscious, one part was the ordinary consciousness, and one part was the superconscious or *aumakua*. Long believed that the conscious, the "middle self," generated the purpose of prayer. He also found that the path to the superconscious was through the unconscious, and that only the unconscious could generate the *mana*, the power, that the superconscious needed to do its work of manifestation. Long's "Huna" is one of the few views of sacrifice in which all the parties need each other. It is an ecology of offering.

While Long emphasized that praying for yourself was acceptable, all his Huna prayers included a wish for the well-being of others. To wish so, he said, was to become allied with the Higher Selves of those beings.

> But first there is a ritual before we present the prayer. The middle self does its part by meditating on and affirming love for the High Self, which the low self builds into powerful emotion. The middle self directs the drive toward the High Self until the contact is made. The *gift* of mana is then made to the High Self for its own high purposes of service and world betterment.
>
> After that, the command is held over the low self to send on the continuing mana flow the picture we have so carefully built of what we wish to have brought to pass for us.
>   — Max Freedom Long[95]

The low self creates the *mana* or energy for offering by visualization or deep breathing, so the energy comes from a surplus of energy rather than depleting the person praying. Long also discovered that it was necessary to invite a return flow after the offering of *mana.*

E ho'o helele'i pa ua pomaikai,
Let the rain of blessings fall!

"When the prayer action is over, it has been found by experience that, for some reason or other, it is also necessary to invite the return flow of mana — mana raised to the High-Self level of power and purity which can heal and bless. The kahunas asked, *'Let the rain of blessings fall.'* We must do the same. It seems to be part of the act of opening the door to the help of the Aumakuas so we may have the aid they are forbidden to give unless their presence is recognized and their aid requested. Always, without exception, we should make this formal ending to prayer if an offering of mana is sent to the High Selves."[96]

This pattern of offering and then request may seem strange, but Jesus used the same pattern in the Lord's Prayer. When he said, "Thy will be done," he was offering (as Gethsemane showed) his whole being. Then he asked for very concrete daily bread, not only for himself but for us.

 ## The Tantric Use of Desire

In the woods near the Great Lakes a teacher turns to her class of students. Most of them have been with her for years. She has taught them to take energy and circulate it through their bodies with their breaths. Now she instructs them to sit in groups of three to learn a form of "heart-work," using the particular power and energy of the heart.

After settling down and aligning their bodies into comfort, they are to begin breathing deep into their abdomens. They join themselves in their minds with "wisdom presence," the field of Buddha awareness from which individual bodhisattvas come to assist beings in such kind deeds as this blessing practice. After they have done so for a while, they are to begin to draw energy in from above and below themselves at the same time, and to let it mix in their hearts. Finally, each threesome allows that energy to flow into the space in front of them. They are to create a new heart in that space, says the teacher, and to invite those in need of help into that heart. The students begin to murmur to each other as they bring names to the heart-space they have created in front of them.

Julie Henderson is teaching her students a path of energy.[97] Because she is a tantrika, she works with energy and awareness. Because she is a Mahayana Buddhist, the work is dedicated to the welfare of all beings, "even the grumpy ones." All the Tibetan ceremonies and vestments, statues and chanting and incense, have as their goals the liberation and benefit of us (the humans, hungry ghosts, demons, animals, titans, and gods) who spin compulsively through unenlightened experience.

But what is specific about Tantra, and where (the gentle reader must be wondering) is the sex part? Desire is one of the energies that tantrics work with, but not the only one. There are also the energies of anger, jealousy, pride, even of ignorance itself. Each of the five Buddha families that are seen in Tibetan mandalas arise from the purification of one of the five great vices. So Amitabha (for instance) is a bodhisattva who has sworn to rescue and bring to a good rebirth any being who calls on him. His compassion is a transformation of desire.

Let all of your loving be for the sake of all beings.

There is a saying that the three great schools of Buddhism are three responses to the poisons inherent in the circle of life and death. The Theravadan learns by austerity and meditation to avoid and remove the poisons; the Mahayanist swears to rescue others who have been poisoned by them; and the tantric Vajrayanist takes those poisons and, with care and great skill, turns them into medicine for all beings. You can tell that it was a Vajrayanist who said this, but it expresses the intention of the Tantra: To take all things and incorporate them into liberation and rescue.

Sounds like great libertinage, doesn't it, to bring your favorite vices into your spiritual path? Ah, but there's the rub — you are not to be their slave, but to offer them. When wracked with desire, you are neither to deny it nor to act it out — but to offer it. The ache from these desires can become very great unless you learn to generate more space in which to let them move (again: without acting them out, unless that embodiment of desire is appropriate) — and that space and movement become part of the offering as well.

When allowed to move in sufficient space, with the intention of the good of all beings and their liberation, these energies become a fire of delight. Constantly offering that fire becomes a tantric prayer for all beings.

Pouring into the self-fire
Already made bright by the offering
of what I should do and what I should not have done,
with my mind as the ladle
along the spinal path
constantly
I offer the turning of the senses
— Vamamarga Tantra III[98]

The energies offered may have many names. As one of the most accomplished tantric masters of the current generation, the Gyalwang Drukpa, observed, the energies need not necessarily be sexual. The statues of embracing Tibetan deities represent the tension and attraction between all opposites, of which sexual desire is only one example (and one with which we in our culture are particularly obsessed, said the lama).

At first, of course, the fire is so intense that you can think of nothing but offering it outwards. But as it becomes more customary (and if you drink enough water!) the ripples of delight become more subtle and more easy to experience without burning. You can then bring those who need help into that field of moving pleasure and allow it to move through them. These waves of delight become what you offer to others, both those who are present and those who are distant in space and time.

You may practice with a tantric partner. As the joy-ripple becomes familiar, you find it arising any time that pleasure and delight begin. Sunsets, small flowers, a laughing dog, any of these can become the trigger for a state of delight that can then be offered for all beings.

 ## Eros in the West

Though it seems that Tantra is a strange path from Asia, it is also known in the West. In Plato's *Symposium* we find that Socrates was taught by Diotima, a priestess who was famous for delaying a great plague for ten years. She taught Socrates a practice that is called "Love" in the puritan translations we have in English. In Greek it is simply *Eros*, "Desire." That desire begins with the hunger for one lovely body, said Diotima, and eventually leads one to perceive Beauty itself. But the desire, the yearning, never goes away at any step of the climb. It is what carries the seeker up from stage to stage.[99]

> Though if you want to know the Truth
> I can so clearly see that God has made love with you
> And the whole universe is germinating
> Inside your belly.
> — Hafiz[100]

This path of desire is found in Judaism (consider the Song of Songs), Islam, and Christianity. We are familiar with the love poetry of Islam in Rumi and Hafiz. But few people have seen the "Hymns of Yearning" of the Christian teacher Hierotheus: "When we talk of yearning [*Eros* or desire], whether this be in God or an angel, in the mind or in the spirit or in nature, we should think of a unifying and co-mingling power which moves the superior to provide for the subordinate, peer to be in communion with peer, and subordinate to return to the superior and the outstanding."[101]

The tantric practice based in desire and the flow of energy is every bit as available for the conservative married or celibate Westerner as it is for the experimenter with Eastern religions. All that is necessary is to take yearning and delight and offer them for the good of all. You yearn for your lover: remember the Song of Songs and offer that yearning to God. Offer it not as a sin, but as a delight. You make love: offer the love and pleasure and the ecstasy of orgasm. You see a beautiful tree: offer the beauty. You see a small butterfly: offer the intense joy. At work you make a perfect spreadsheet: remember that Diotima included business-people among lovers, and offer the accomplishment. At each moment of joy, small or large, offer it. Allow the joy and desire to move and change (when confined, desire burns) and then offer it to the One who loves the cosmos, for the sake of all beings.

The practice of offering suffering, merit, and delight are specific forms of prayer for others. The practice of offering itself may be the prerequisite of all prayer for other beings. In it we genuinely turn our attention to others, away from our beloved me-space. Dr. Henderson says, "For the first several years of our lives we spend a great deal of attention learning to notice the sensations of being a body. It is the main way that we make a sense of self. This vortex of attention to our particular location is necessarily narcissistic. Offering implies, at least conceptually, the reality of other beings. Continuity of any generous practice has as one of its principal effects a broadened and broadening range of perception, through which the reality of other beings becomes more and more immediate and 'felt' by us."

BRINGING WISDOM
AND COMPASSION
TO OTHERS

One of the students in our weekly consultation was profoundly uncomfortable. When we asked why, she described a deep despair and solitude that nothing could break. But when she moved from her chair, the feeling lifted immediately. When others sat in her chair, they too felt a desperate alienation. I tried it: it was like looking through a telescope the wrong way. Everyone was distant and untouchable, and "that is how things are." The feeling was in the room, a despairing and inevitable isolation. Another student felt an infant presence, dark like a room with no light in it, and it seemed that the despair was coming from him.[102]

As we wondered where the wild, grieving infant spirit that seemed to be among us had come from, another presence could be felt. It was a tall woman, black as the night sky. To my mind she seemed like the ancient portrayals of Isis, who wore the dark night as a cloak. Our teacher said she was T'hröma Nagmo, the wrathful Black Mother of Tibetan Buddhism. The feeling about her was not of anger, though she was dealing with the rage of the infant. It was of spaciousness and resourcefulness.

In a set of quick showings, she demonstrated to the tiny infant the kinds of spaces through which he could move.

His suffering was not inevitable, she seemed to say, because he could escape through this tunnel in experience, or this one, or this one. In a flash the child's presence was gone. He had taken one of the pathways she had shown, and was liberated. The oppression lifted instantly from the room.

And she too was gone. Behind she left only a surprised awareness that, even in the most desperately trapped situation, help can come.

 ## Learning from Buddhists

For many years I have kept company with Buddhists. My spiritual teacher is Dr. Julie Henderson, with whom the reader has become familiar throughout these pages. She has been uniformly kind and has repeatedly invited me to experience what the Buddhists texts talk about.

It seems to me that Buddhism is not primarily a religion, but an experiential psychology and a philosophical background. Judaism, Christianity, and Islam grew up around the Mediterranean. The high culture in terms of which the Semitic religions needed to explain themselves was descended from Orpheus, Pythagoras, Parmenides, Diotima, Socrates, Plato, and Aristotle, the tutor of conquering Alexander. They had a view of distinct selves, permanent realities, hidden but real essences that intellect could find, and lawful cosmologies. All of modern Western thought has been raised upon that view.

Buddhism on the other hand tends to see interconnected beings, the unreality of apparent separation and independent selves, constant change, and a self-enforcing law of moral consequences. Asian countries grew up with this

Buddhist understanding as the high culture rather than our Greek view.

Buddhism has evolved with one great grace: It has progressively rejected the belief that some must suffer for others to be well. The world was not a "zero-sum game" in which the winners' gains came from the losses of the losers. Instead, Buddhism insisted that everyone must win in the long run.

In India, for instance, it rejected the caste system and welcomed all classes in the Buddhist community. In a country in which a person's meaning came from the social station into which they were born, this was a powerful social gospel. Women were practitioners and monastics, and (at least among the early tantrics) leaders.[103]

It also included non-human beings in its plan of salvation. Although human beings had particular advantages in approaching enlightenment, Buddhism was preached to all entities. Animals, ghosts, gods, and demons were all invited to accept the teaching, and tradition says than many of them did. The belief that we migrate through many bodies never took root in the West, though Pythagoras held it.[104] Buddhism held it strongly and spread it throughout Asia. The doctrine meant that anyone might occupy any kind of body, so none could be ignored.

A new kind of hero arose, the volunteer savior. In Buddhism people can take vows that they will not accept their own freedom from karma and reincarnation until *all* beings are free. By taking this vow, a person undertakes an ages-long practice of wisdom and compassion for others.

These two themes, of salvation for all beings and of voluntary saviors, move within a background belief that there are no unchanging essences, that all things are impermanent and nothing is isolated. This doctrine actually gives rise to many hopeful consequences: that no being is

1. Our life is shaped by our mind; we become what we think. Suffering follows an evil thought as the wheel of the cart follows the oxen that draw it.

2. Our life is shaped by our mind, we become what we think. Joy follows a pure thought like a shadow that never leaves.

3. "He was angry with me, he attacked me, he defeated me, he robbed me" — those who dwell on such thoughts will never be free from hatred.

4. For hatred can never put an end to hatred, love alone can. This is the unalterable law.

— Siddhartha Gautama, *The Dhammapada*

irretrievably lost, that no being is beyond helpful contact, and that it behooves us to bless all.

When I think of Buddhism, I often think of how the Christianity in which I was raised would differ if it were flavored with Buddhist rather than Greek philosophy. I wonder what would have happened if the context of the expanding Semitic religions had been a Buddhist rather than a Greek world. The question is not entirely fantasy: some Christians did move to China in the seventh century. Christianity evolved within that milieu until the Holy Spirit was referred to as "The Cool Breeze" and Christ in heaven was seen surrounded by bodhisattvas.[105]

There are powerful ways of praying for others that come out of Buddhism. *Metta* (the first described here) appeals to everyone who hears about it. The next two, based in Mahayana metaphysics and Tantric experience, make sense to me now; but I have to admit they might not have done so before I encountered Dr. Henderson.

The Gift of the Theravada

The Theravada, oldest of Buddhism's many forms, gives us the form of blessing known as *Metta* or "Lovingkindness." The Buddha said: "He [a monk] continually relates to those in one direction with a mind endowed with love, then likewise to those in the second, the third, and the fourth; and in the same way to the beings upward, downward and across. He continually relates everywhere, equally, to the entire world of beings with a mind endowed with love — a mind that is untroubled, free from enmity, vast, enlarged and measureless."

> May all be well and secure,
> May all beings be happy!
>
> Whatever living creatures there be,
> Without exception, weak or strong,
> Long, huge or middle-sized,
> Or short, minute or bulky,
>
> Whether visible or invisible,
> And those living far or near,
> The born and those seeking birth,
> May all beings be happy!
>
> —Karaniya Metta Sutta[106]

The blessing of *metta* is a wish that others be well, that they escape suffering, that they be joyous, and that they experience equanimity — the "Four Immeasurables." Gautama Shakyamuni (the historical Buddha of twenty-five hundred years ago) knew that this form of blessing changed the person who practiced it. The Buddha gave a list of eleven personal benefits, here in Thich Nhat Hanh's version:

The practitioner sleeps well.

Upon waking, he or she feels well and light in his heart.

He does not have unpleasant dreams.

She is well-liked by many people. She feels at ease with everyone. Others, especially children, like to be near her.

He is dear to the nonhuman species: birds, fish, elephants, squirrels. Species that are visible and invisible like to be near him.

She is supported and protected by gods and goddesses.

He is protected from fire, poison, and the sword. He does not need to make any special effort to avoid them.

She reaches meditative concentration easily.

His face is bright and clear.

At the time of death, her mind is clear.

He is reborn in the Brahma Heaven, where he can continue the practice, because there is already a Sangha of those practicing the Four Immeasurable Minds.[107]

The Buddha also knew that *metta* had effects on others, and it is reported that he used it himself: "Once the Buddha was returning from his almsround together with his retinue of monks. As they were nearing the prison, in consideration of a handsome bribe from Devadatta, the Buddha's evil and ambitious cousin, the executioner let loose the fierce elephant Nalagiri, which was used for the execution of criminals. As the intoxicated elephant rushed towards the Buddha trumpeting fearfully, the Buddha projected powerful thoughts of metta towards it. Venerable Ananda, the Buddha's attendant, was so deeply concerned about the Buddha's safety that he ran in front of the Buddha to shield him, but the Buddha asked him to stand aside since the projection of love itself was quite sufficient. The impact of the Buddha's metta-radiation was so immediate and overwhelming that by the time the animal neared the Buddha it was completely tamed as though a drunken wretch had suddenly become sober by the magical power of a spell. The tusker, it is said, bowed down in reverence in the way trained elephants do in a circus."[108]

When monks meditating in the forest were disturbed by spirits, the Buddha taught them the *Metta Sutta*. When the monks practiced it, the spirits were pacified,[109] and they too began to practice.[110] Metta is a form of protection in which the one who is attacking is not harmed but blessed.

Buddhist psychology tends to be straightforward and practical. The instruction is to bless both *all* beings and also specific local persons, to begin with the easy-to-bless, and later to work with the less agreeable. Teachers encourage practitioners to begin by blessing themselves and friends before moving on to the more difficult people they don't care about, or to enemies. The great Theravadan compiler Buddhaghosa suggested beginning with a small area — one house — and then to extend the practice house by house until one can develop lovingkindness "up to the world-sphere, and even beyond that."[111]

Metta is one of the simplest blessings one can find. It does not require a theological position. It was apparently older than Buddhism. In India, for instance, it was shared by Buddhists and such Hindus as Patañjali. *Metta* has been presented in the West in a secular form by Swiss-Czech psychotherapist Mirko Fryba, who refers to it as "strategies of sympathy."[112]

In a Christian context *metta* seems particularly appropriate. Christians are instructed to love and to bless even the enemy, but it is not easy to do so. There has been much theological instruction in the "vertical" connection to God. That is only the first of the Two Great Commandments, the second being to love others as yourself.[113] A Christian introduction to the practice of *metta* says that "It helps you grow in the horizontal direction toward all."[114]

God is *metta*, and the one who abides in *metta* abides in God, and God abides in that one. — cf. 1 John 4:16

The word *metta* in Pali (the language of the earliest Buddhist scriptures) seems to be exactly the word that Bible translators would use if they were translating the Greek word *agape,* or love. If the New Testament were written in Pali, all references to love would be rendered by this Buddhist blessing-word.

 ## *Becoming Wisdom and Compassion to Help with Suffering*

If you are simply wishing beings well, there is no problem. But if you attempt to make things "all better," or to take on suffering by yourself, you can be overwhelmed.

There is a practice called "taking refuge" that is part of becoming a Buddhist. You say, "I take refuge in the Buddha, I take refuge in the Dharma [the teaching], I take refuge in the Samgha [the community]." This is more than just formula of admission into a religion. Some people attempt to take on huge suffering without first resting in wisdom and compassion. "What are you *doing,* touching suffering without taking refuge first?" asks Dr. Henderson.

> One way of describing refuge is as a connection to the
> protective, developmental presence of wisdom and love;
> refuge is traditionally followed by *bodhicitta* or wishing
> beings well. When we're prepared in this way by refuge, by
> the connection to beings who are already awake, then the
> feeling encounter with suffering is not so overwhelming.
> Some practitioners move too soon to engage the suffering
> of beings, without the proper context. If you don't know
> that wisdom and compassion are real and available, it's
> virtually impossible to feel the suffering of other beings
> without deciding that our being at all is a bad thing.
>
> — Julie Henderson

"Taking refuge" means going within wisdom and compassion *before* connecting with the suffering of other beings. We are not dependent on just our own resources — we can rest within beings who have far greater wisdom and compassion than we yet have.

Within? Yes. Tantric Buddhism teaches its students many of the same forms of prayer that other religions have. But it also has the surprising practice of "identifying with the wisdom being." A student imagines one of the wisdom beings (buddhas or bodhisattvas) in front, and then brings that wisdom being closer and closer until the wisdom being surrounds the student, specifically so their energy is within the wisdom being, and their heart is within the heart of the wisdom being. Then the student dissolves into the wisdom being — energy into energy, heart into heart — allowing all difference to vanish. The identification is as complete as possible. Finally the student will allow the wisdom being to dissolve into the openness from which all things — even wisdom beings — arise.

There is no essential boundary that separates one being from another. This is one of the meanings of the Buddhist doctrine of "no self." Our view of the self in the West makes it hard to imagine two selves merging this way. But while the Buddhists acknowledge that such merging is not ordinary, it is certainly not impossible. The student uses this lack of essential separation to deliberately *become* the wisdom being. The Buddhist wisdom beings invite it, and there is even a name for the strong feeling of confidence that arises from the practice: "Diamond pride." Dr. Henderson says the steps of the identification are to be aware *of* the wisdom being, then to be aware *in* the wisdom being, and finally to be aware *as* the wisdom being.

When we enter the awareness of the wisdom being, we realize that we were never distinct, and that all beings with whom we interact are also wisdom beings.

"Don't just pretend to be the deity, Heruka for instance, as I have already said. That is not what you are doing when you visualize yourself as the deity. Instead, you should feel from the depths of your being that you *are* Heruka, that you and he are an inseparable unity. The more you cultivate this unity, the more powerful your experience of transformation will become."[115]

If we enter into the awareness of a wisdom being, we become aware of openness, compassion, and a lack of barriers, because a wisdom being is aware *as* those things.

 ## Receiving Wisdom

If you work with a lama, you may be given a *yidam*, a wisdom being particularly appropriate for your temperament. The selection of a *yidam* for students is one of the skills of being a teacher. The teacher in the role of *lama* also transmits the consciousness of that *yidam* to the student, giving a taste and an example of the awareness that the student will learn to develop autonomously later.

Christians, of course, have a *yidam* in Jesus: "That they all may be one; as thou, Father, *art* in me, and I in thee, that they also may be one in us: that the world may believe that thou hast sent me."[116]

The fifteenth chapter of the Gospel of John instructs the Christian to undertake just this practice. The most explicit invitation is when Jesus speaks of the vine and the branches. The vine includes the branches. Jesus seems to be saying that his disciples are simply to become extensions of what he is. "I am the vine, ye [are] the branches: He that abideth in me, and I in him, the same bringeth forth much fruit: for without me ye can do nothing."[117]

Jesus tell his followers to "abide in me" over and over again in John 15. And the practice is not optional: "If a man abide not in me, he is cast forth as a branch, and is withered; and men gather them, and cast [them] into the fire, and they are burned."[118]

 ## Blessing With Wisdom

What would it mean to pray for someone else while merged with and in-formed by a wisdom being? To become the Holy is to accept the power and wisdom of the Holy, so it is from that position that we work. That participation/identification gives an extraordinarily different viewpoint when we work for the benefit of others. In Buddhist practice it means that you take the issue with you into your merging with Tara or Vajrapani or Avalokiteshvara or the Medicine Buddha, and then the power and the wisdom and the compassion of that wisdom being addresses the issue you've brought with you.

I have had the experience of identifying with one of the great wisdom beings once. First there was a great sense of expansion, and then of relaxation. Then there was a sense that there were no barriers — I simply floated in the awareness. I was doing distant work on a particularly difficult person (read: someone who was not doing what I wanted), and when I looked at him through this huge viewpoint, he suddenly enlarged and became a fierce Heruka Buddha. In Buddhist terms, his innate Buddha-nature became visible to me. The independence and don't-mess-with-me quality was still there, but it was integrated into the wrathful wisdom being's compassion and determination to make things right. I could feel, like a shadow within a bright light, that his "ordinary aspect" was moving as well, and changing to match this expanded reality. All this perception and appreciation came to me because I was identified for the moment with a wisdom being.

The characteristics of certain wisdom beings makes them particularly appropriate for certain kinds of work. For example, Red Tara (whose mantra is OM TARE TAM SOHA) is associated with strong, fierce energies.[119] As a bodhisattva, she is committed to helping beings to transform those energies into good circumstances. You could just ask for her help, which is a common practice in the Buddhist world. But you can also identify with her and collaborate in the work she already does, and focus it on issues you are concerned about.

Our teacher used this practice at an Australian retreat during the fire season there. She and her students repeatedly did a Red Tara practice to help the firefighters contain the blaze. First they identified with Tara, then drew in the energy of the fire and radiated it out again as coolness.

The temperature dropped ten to twelve degrees, and the air grew damp.

Could you use this identification with powerful beings to do bad things? It would be hard, because these beings are exactly the opposite of bad-thing-doers. Over uncounted lifetimes they have worked to develop positive qualities to help others. Their qualities resist being used to harm. They resist so strongly, in fact, that if we did try to use them to harm others, the contact would likely change us for the better us rather than damage the other.

 ## The Gift of Space

Buddhism values space. While other traditions emphasize the fullness of being, Buddhism has stressed its openness. There is room to move. What was constraining, closing in, entrapping, is cut through. The great image of liberation is the open sky, and the metaphor is commonly used for both this open state of mind and for compassion.

The tangled busyness of life, from the most terrible sufferings to the most lovely pleasures, is seen as arising from and subsiding into the openness that underlies them.

> KYE HO! Wonderful!
> Magical displays arise in the sky
> Through the dynamism of the sky itself.
> Arising spontaneously as transformations of sky.[120]

In this sky, space-traversing Dakinis and "wrathful" (or change-making) wisdom beings dance, peaceful wisdom beings rest in perfect poise, and the lights of emancipation flash from the free to the still-entangled.

The essence of that freedom is open spaciousness. Buddhists seek to have spacious souls. The words for happiness (*sukha*) and suffering (*duhkha*) etymologically mean "good space" and "bad space." So it is not a surprise that one Buddhist way of praying for others involves giving space.

Let your heart be as wide and clear as the winter sky. . . .

— Bairo Tulku Rinpoche

They begin by "finding," mentioned in the chapter about keeping company.

A shy and therefore anonymous member of our group discussed the experience of finding: "It is like being in a space in which distance is fluid, but there is still location and shape. When you "find" someone, they usually feel like a thickening or a knot in the space. Each person has different feelings to them, so they are not all the same. But people have location and the qualities of them are gathered around that location."

One time Dr. Henderson asked us to find several people, one after another, and we did. Then, at the end, she invited us to find her teacher. He was not there! There was no thickening and clustering of qualities in the way we'd experienced with other people. Instead there was a vast and roomy space, with just a little hint of irony in it. It took us a while to realize that that roomy space *was* the lama we were looking for.[121]

Lama in Tibetan means both the individual persons called lamas, "and the spacious compassionate awakeness without limit itself, which is the inherent natural state of all beings. . . . "

When a person is a space rather than the contents of a space, it is possible to be inside them with great ease.

Pavlina von Metzler, one of Dr. Henderson's European students, calls this "Lamaspace" — a place where one can be easily, a safe and helpful space.

Dr. Henderson talks about nesting spaces that fit within each other like bowls fitting within bowls. It's a little like that. One could guess that there are other Lamaspaces inside of which her teacher's Lamaspace nestles, and so on outward to the great Buddhas who provide sanctuary for billions of beings. We are made out of space and so are they — but they know it and use that spaciousness to provide refuge for others. And they seem to enjoy doing so.

Those who give space, whether accomplished lamas or beginners, do not give an open emptiness. Instead they give just the kind of space that the being seems to need. Perhaps it's just a little more room. Perhaps it is a containing space, to shield one from the agoraphobia of infinity. Perhaps it is the multiple-path space of alternatives — new ways to go when it seemed that there were no choices available — as Th'röma offered the entrapped infant. The space is nearly always shaped in some way, shaped to combine openness with what the receiver needs.

The practice is often combined with the merging with Lama, to allow the awareness of Lama to shape the space being offered. Von Metzler says: "All I do is to let Lama within me, and I relax in all the directions I can. I let the situation be in the Lama space and it dissolves there. The heart grows more open and the pain I often felt before is not there. Strangely, my feeling is that in this way I am much more of help.... "

We tend to think of ourselves as separate and exclusive. If I am sitting in this chair, no one else can sit here at the same time. But there is a second opinion within Christianity. God is both a Person and That within whom "we live and move and have our being"[122] as the King James Version says. We exist *within* God. Renaissance Platonist Ficino said, "Spirit is spacious."[123] Spirit is room to live and develop, room to move and change, and room to be. We can give the gift of openness, which we inherit because of Where we live. The Buddhists remind us to unite with our Teacher and offer this gift to all beings.

THE EXPERIENCE OF UNIFICATION

How can there be a hierarchy among methods of prayer? I have to admit my own prejudice: The "high end" of praying for others is Unification. In this family of methods, no one tries to make anything happen. Instead, we unify with the person we pray for, and also with the Good — a Good beyond the highest good we can find.

The experience of Unification is like a vast expansion, like coming out into an open and friendly space after being shut up in a small smoky room. The problem that brought you to prayer, its difficulty and even your own personality, are part of the smallness of the room you were in. The huge, freeing space you enter contains an Infinity of Solution, in the words of Marion Weinstein.[124] Everything becomes well: in the context we have entered, there is no way that anything could be wrong.

The larger space, where created things come from, would be a terrible place if it were not friendly. But it is friendly, loving, and very caring. If you carry your troubles and those of the ones you care about to that place, they dissolve. When you return to ordinary experience, the world you come back to is different.

Unlike the types of prayer in which God remains a fellow being — separate from us and possibly one of many — in the experience of Unification, God is not another being. God is the context for all beings and is necessarily unique.

Prayers of Unification are somewhat like pattern praying, except that Unification means to climb beyond even the positive qualities of the Holy. It's impossible to say anything accurate about the Highlands of God, report the mystical traditions of Judaism, Christianity, and Islam. That claim reflects the common experience of the tiny, magical "blackouts" during prayer and meditation that are associated with the greatest healing for ourselves and others.

No one can do anything about moving or changing Spirit, influencing It or bribing It. There is nothing to do but *let* It envelop you, *let* It pick you up, *let* It dominate you, *let* Its will be done in you, and then you make of yourself a transparency through which the light that is already present within you can shine.   —Joel Goldsmith[125]

When the practitioners of Transcendental Meditation did research about their form of mantra practice, they discovered many health benefits for the practitioners and social benefits for the cities and environment in which they meditated. More thorough research revealed that the most intense effects came when the practitioner had entered a mental silence in which even the mantra went away. It was during those moments of ineffable quiet that the positive effects for the whole practice were taking place. It was in the silence that the stress reduction (for instance) actually occurred.[126]

Buddhists speak of emptiness. In the famous Heart Sutra, the Bodhisattva of Compassion finds emptiness in all phenomena. When Kindness sought Truth, in other words, Kindness found Selflessness. This lack of self, an absence of intelligible essence, makes it difficult to speak of the selfless state. The same lack of intelligibility means that people of different theologies can meet there. Even those of us who pray within agnosticism, because it's all that is available to us, can turn to this "dark mysticism." It's not necessary to know what God is to seek in this way. You *reach for, listen for, look for* God with all your intensity instead of reasoning about God.

Are these states only for practiced mystics? Or are they open to everyone? In my experience they are accessible, sometimes; and many more people are called to be healing mystics than would believe it.

The anonymous medieval English mystical manual *The Cloud of Unknowing* said: "Lift up thine heart unto God with a meek stirring of love; and mean Himself, and none of His goods. And thereto, look the loath to think on aught but Himself. So that nought work in thy wit, nor in thy will, but only Himself. And do that in thee is to forget all the creatures that ever God made and the works of them; so that thy thought nor thy desire be not directed nor stretched to any of them, neither in general nor in special, but let them be, and take no heed to them."[127]

This practice involves no reaching out to other created beings; nevertheless, it benefits others: "All men living in earth be wonderfully holpen of this work, thou wottest not how. Yea, the souls in purgatory be eased of their pain by virtue of this work. Thyself art cleansed and made virtuous by no work so much."

People in many traditions have found that this bare mysticism, with few doctrines and a simple practice, forms a powerful way to pray for others.

 The Keeler Method

W. Frederic Keeler was an American healer and teacher in the late nineteenth century and the first half of the twentieth century. I've been grateful to Keeler for many years, because he was the first prayer-teacher whose methods I could use.

Keeler was both a Spiritualist and a Unity minister before becoming an independent teacher. He was a curmudgeon with a sense of humor; he rejected affirmations with the question, "Do you believe in lying? For good?" Nor did he believe in wordy explanations. His language grew simpler and more telegraphic throughout his life.

Utterly pragmatic, he earned his living for a while as a coal prospector. And when he taught others his methods of healing, he kept them as minimalist as possible. The secret for him was Unification, but without the great effort that some forms of mysticism enjoin. "There is no struggle in Spirit," he said. "If you find yourself laboring, or struggling, or at all upset, you are not treating."[128]

Divine Love cannot be forced. Stop doing everything. Things do not rest upon us. Forsake egotism in every subtle disguise. We give ourselves, or at least endeavor to give our consciousness, even for a moment, to Divine Love. We are patient about it; we are easy with ourselves in it. Be an observer of it all. Judgment is with the Lord in all things. We bring ourselves and our thoughts into the presence of Divine Love. We associate at least the possibility of Divine Love with all things and with each thing. We learn, in our secret thoughts at least, to live in relationship with the Best. As a result of this, either as a habit or as a specially applied endeavor, we simply find a tremendous result brought about in the daily life experience — health, harmony and success.
— W. Fredric Keeler[129]

Keeler emphasized that healing work is not just floating off into ecstasy, but rather to unite worldly life with the Presence of God and in particular to connect that Presence with the person who is suffering.

"In answer to such a question as 'Wherein do I fail to produce the healing results that I should have?,' I would as a general answer say, 'You are not giving sufficient attention in your treatments to your patient.' The bond of unworried interest in the patient may have been forgotten, and a personal idealization of spiritual things has been permitted to invade the actualities of the treatment. . . . We are not to limit our endeavors to an indulgence in the enjoyments of merely basking in Spirit."[130]

Keeler's work is based on peacefully linking God and the patient in our consciousness: "That connection, itself, is enough to heal. The perfect life is that of living with the Master. The glory is that it requires no science, no learning. One does not prepare for it. One does it. . . . Should trouble come into our lives, we take that trouble to the Master. Placing that trouble before the Master dissolves it, heals it. When trouble is dissolved by intelligence, it is healed. The Master is not only intelligent. He is INTELLIGENCE."[131]

 The Path of Love

For some, the path to Unification is the path of love.

Sister Colette has been a member of the Poor Clares since Richard Nixon was president. Her Franciscan order of Roman Catholic nuns is enclosed and contemplative. The relationship between the nuns and Jesus is particularly intimate, because each one is married to Christ. Each wears a wedding ring that she receives when she makes her final vows. The words in a pamphlet about the order are frankly romantic: "And Christ is a Lover who will never fail her, never desert her, never grow tired of her. Unlike a woman entering human wedlock, the novice making the marriage vows of religion can perfectly forecast the future as far as her Bridegroom is concerned. He will be forever faithful, loving, devoted to her. With His grace, she will be so to Him. And out of this union of God and creature will issue blessings for all the world."[132]

When I spoke to Sister Colette the first time, she put it very directly: "Jesus is our Spouse. We do not get to walk down the beach hand in hand with Him, but He is."

I guess being in a state of prayer you're totally focused on God and on His praise, and then the rest of your life flows from that.
— Sister Colette

The center of Franciscan spirituality is love, and Franciscan thinkers focus on that communion. Sister Colette has spent many years thinking about the God of love, and has distilled her experience down into extremely compressed chains of reasoning: She says: "God is love. And therefore to pray is to be in communion with that love. So to be in communion with love is to learn to love — to learn what love is, to learn what it is to be loved. And all that's involved in prayer, because prayer is primarily adoration. Prayer is primarily praise of Him with Whom we pray."

God is, she says, "your very source, your very center." Learning to love could be difficult for a creature, except for the great positive paradox: " . . . you love by being loved. So the people who have loved you have taught you a lot about praying."

In this context of love, prayer is not a utilitarian act. It is instead an act of communion. When Sister Colette prays for someone, she simply thinks of them during the time that she is immersed in love with God. She often has a picture of the person she is praying for in her breviary, sometimes surrounded with Scripture quotations. "The connection with the person I am praying for could best be described as empathy, experiencing what they are feeling. I do not have many extraordinary experiences. They come into focus, and then (at a certain point) the focus moves on."

But the emphasis in her prayer is not on the person for whom she is praying or on their need. The focus instead is on God, and specifically (I think) on God as spouse. The person in need can be brought into this intimacy, an existing communion between Sister Colette and God. That relationship is full of Love and praise, and they are therefore bathed in it.

Sister Colette declines to measure results. While she has no quarrel with those who believe otherwise, she does not wish to do prayer tests: "I do not feel it is appropriate to test God, because prayer is a loving relationship. I do not want to test One I love."

Nor is feeling good a basis for evaluating prayer. Some days, she says, you may not feel anything. Other days she feels His loving presence in a very tangible way. But whether you feel something or not, you pray. She says, with a small laugh, "When you love someone you don't always have to feel good."

Nevertheless, the prayers of the Poor Clares have a good reputation among those for whom they pray: "But people say that they ask us to pray and things happen right away, that they're asking for. Some people are sure they want the Poor Clares to pray because (and here she laughed) it always happens."

Prayer With Glenn Clark

Glenn Clark was a Presbyterian layman and college professor who helped create a revival of prayer in the mainline Protestant churches. He led thousands of people in very personal prayer trainings at his Camps Farthest Out during the middle of the twentieth century.

> Prayer with Jesus is very simple. You take your own or your brother's need deep into your heart, and identify yourself with it. Then, forgetting your brother and yourself, as best you can, and, above all, forgetting your trouble, turn completely in thought to God and rise into that high consciousness of oneness with the Father, through the consciousness (or name) of your oneness with Christ, and having risen to that high place, you pray until the Peace of God comes upon you. Then your prayer is answered.
>
> — Glenn Clark

Glenn Clark was certainly aware of many forms of prayer. He had a reputation as an effective intercessor so strong that people called out to him to pray for them, as we discussed earlier. But of this form of prayer by becoming lost in God he said: "This is the secret of my own power in prayer, and herein lies a deep mystery, a mystery to myself and to my friends, a mystery that until now, I have found it very difficult to explain."[133] Clark would take the troubles about which he was praying with him as he went into prayer — he made those troubles his own — and then he abandoned them in the high places of God. It was, he said, like taking a rug out and cleaning it with dry snow: when he had swept all the concern he had away, he knew that the troubles he was praying about were also gone.

Disappearing in God

I spoke with Imam Bilal Hyde, an American convert to Islam. Imam Hyde is a community leader among Sufis, as well as an orthodox *Sunni* practitioner. He told me hat the most common prayer for others in Islam is the *Fatiha*, the first chapter of the Quran.

Imam Hyde prays this prayer in the original Arabic, as do most Muslims. Since I didn't understand why he preferred to pray using this set formula, he explained to me that the ritual is part of a larger practice, or goal.

The key to all other spiritual activity, he said, is called *fanā*. It means "annihilation." It's something like approaching emptiness. "The reason for a formula, or a ritual, is so that one's personality is completely uninvolved in the process. So you're not thinking. Or making it up. Or even feeling. You completely disappear.... So, this is the first step, to effective intercession, is that you disappear into the formula that you repeat.

"It's almost like someone else is praying," the Imam went on. "You're watching, someone else is praying. Rumi is full of these images 'like a sugar cube in tea,' " laughed the Imam "completely disappeared.

"Then instead of *your* prayer for someone else, it's a prayer ascending out of the deepest heart, beyond the personality, and it ascends — this is why we [and here Imam Hyde made the palms-up gesture that Muslims around the world make while praying] like this — it ascends from the heart, out through the palms, and it ascends out into the universe."

147

AL-FATIHA: "THE OPENING"

"Bismillah Ar-rahman Ar-rahim, Alhamdulillah rab'l alamin, Ar-rahman Ar-rahim. Meliki yaum adeen, iyaka nabudu wa iyaka nesta'in, ehdina isaratul al-mustaqim, Saratul-ladhina anamta aleyhum ghayr'l maghdubi aleyhim waladalim"

A Sufi translation by Imam Hyde:

We begin in the Name of God, Everlasting Mercy, Infinite Compassion, Praise be to God, Loving Lord of all the worlds. Everlasting Mercy, Infinite Compassion. Eternal Strength of every living being, Whose Majestic Power embraces us on the day of the great return. Only you do we adore, and to you alone do we cry for help. Guide us, Oh God, on the path of Perfect Harmony, the path of those whom you have blessed with the gifts of Peace, Joy, Serenity and Delight, the path of those who have not been brought down by anger, the path of those who have not been lost along the way. Amin. So be it.

Imam Hyde is aware how contrary this removal of self is to our culture's habit of trying to put personal feeling into prayer. Instead of helping the prayer and the one making it, Imam Hyde's Sufi tradition finds that these personalizations impede the process of connection with God and of intercession. They become a veil, and that veil must be removed.

In this path *fanā* is not an abstract theological idea, but a concrete practice that allows the practitioner to become empty of those good and not-so-good feelings. The goal is to become what the Quran said of Muhammad — because the Prophet is the supreme model for humans — to become *Rahmat il-alamin,* "a Mercy to All the Worlds."[134]

The fact that he did not make up the *Fatiha* is part of the way Imam Hyde can let go of his personality in the situation: "That prayer doesn't really come from me," he said. "I didn't make it up. So somehow, repeating those words purifies my feelings, where I get emptier, and emptier, and emptier, and emptier. . . . "

He is visualizing that person, the whole time, as he's repeating and at the same time watching, he gets emptier and emptier. "The point is it has an effect on me, I know, that's for sure; and *insh'allah* — it means, 'If God wills' — it has an effect, a positive effect on that person."

The *fanā* that arises from using a formulaic prayer is what makes intercessory prayer work for Imam Hyde.

I would say, pretty much, that the degree of *fanā* determines the efficacy of the prayer, or we say, *bi ithn 'allah,* "except for God wills," you know? Except for God wills. Disappearing, I would say, is the key to this kind of prayer.

Jewish Mystical Ascension

Mystical Judaism has a complex tradition of ascent to God; it uses language like that of *The Cloud of Unknowing.* And this is no surprise: Jewish, Christian, and Muslim mysticism have all been powerfully influenced by Platonic experience. Ascending to God in Jewish mysticism involves passing through three stages. Their Hebrew names are created by saying less and less: *Ayn Sof Or* ("Limitless Light"), then *Ayn Sof* (the "Unlimited"), and finally *Ayn* (or simply "Not"). Chassidic Judaism makes much of the *Yesh,* the "what is," arising from and returning to the *Ayn,* or the "Not" of God.

> Nothing can change from one thing to another [without first losing its original identity]. Thus, for example, before an egg can grow into a chicken, it must first cease totally to be an egg. Each thing must lose its original identity before it can be something else.
>
> Therefore, before a thing is transformed into something else, it must first come to the level of Nothingness.
>
> This is how a miracle comes about, changing the laws of nature. First the thing must be elevated to the Emanation of Nothingness. Influence then comes from that Emanation to produce the miracle. —Aryeh Kaplan[135]

Rabbi Aryeh Kaplan gave more detail of what this means when one is praying for something to happen. As one moves from what is to what is desired, one must move from the apparently solid world of manifestation to the world without manifestation, the *Ayn* that is both where all things come from and That to which they all return.[136] Only in that world of non-being can things change.

And when one passes through the realm of Not, you also become not. But consider the Company you acquire. As Young's literal translation of the Torah says at Genesis 5:24: "And Enoch walketh habitually with God, and he is not, for God hath taken him."[137]

THE CHALLENGES OF PRAYER

Praying for others allows you be with people in very difficult hours, and to have a positive role in good times and bad times. But prayer has its own hard times.

There's the time when you're certain that a judiciously placed curse is called for, because someone or something is just *so* evil. There are moments when you feel like a miracle-worker, and others when you feel responsible for everything in the universe. Sometimes you feel that both you and prayer are failures. The path of this practice is not smooth. There are dark times in soul work

 *Cursing*

I probably don't need to say anything about "cursing," or the use of prayer to hurt or destroy. The only message I would have is this — if you are tempted to curse someone or something because they are bad and deserve it, please remember that they did what they did — that very evil act — with the same feeling of justification. It is a fearful thing to hate, and in the world of prayer it is even more fearful because in that world there are fewer barriers. What you pour out will spill back on you, it seems. More than that, it will flow through you on its way out and it will leave you the cook's portion.

> We often think our own prayers cannot hurt others, but in fact if we pray to get a certain job we are praying against others who also want or need the job. If we pray to land a funding proposal the same holds true. If we pray for our crops we are praying that insects and weeds, parts of creation, should die — unless we are wise enough to pray by loving them all and knowing that we can only bless one another. Or wise enough to pray for what is best, no strings attached.
>
> That is the crux of the matter. This notion that one person's interests (or the best interests of one part of creation human or non-) can be opposed to the best interests of another person or part of creation, is a shaky basis for prayer. — Deborah Klingbeil

That, I think, is why so many spiritual masters have insisted that we respond to hatred with what kindness we can muster. It is said that the Chassidic Rabbi Mikhal gave this command to his sons: "Pray for your enemies that all may be well with them. And should you think that this is not serving God, rest assured that more than all prayers, this is, indeed, the service of God"[138]

> Pray, "Those who pray to hurt can only bless themselves and others," and include your own self in such a prayer, and mean it. . . . — Deborah Klingbeil

We are human, of course, so we launch a curse before we think of it. The only cure is to send blessing after it, to dissolve the curse and clean the air. If we have nothing but anger, we can pray for ourselves. If others have nothing but anger, we can pray for them.

 ## A Few Stumbling Blocks

There are personality quirks you can get from this practice of prayer. In my own life I have seen "over-control" (the sense of too much responsibility), inflation (the sneaking belief that you are personally chosen by God to glow in the dark), the despair of failure and guilt, and the sense of unworthiness.

Overcontrol

After a few successes, a few answered prayers, there can come a sense that you are in charge of the universe and that you have to supervise it personally.

A Religious Science minister I know called it "treating every dog and cat" — the image is of treating every time anything goes past your eyes. Probably that's all right; but if it's combined with the sense that *you* must make everything right, then you are in trouble. You are slowly suffocated by a sense of responsibility, a sense that you must personally take care of everything that happens. Since there is always something that needs work, this sense will take all the pleasure out of life. If you take time off, you think you are neglecting someone who needs you.

I wish I knew a quick cure for this sense of extreme responsibility, but I don't think there is one. Mahayana Buddhism is known for the bodhisattvas, persons who have taken vows not to go into nirvana until all the beings in the universe have gone before them. In other words, they have promised to remain in this position of over-responsibility forever. But there are stories of the un-believably accomplished bodhisattvas just plain hitting the wall. Avalokiteshvara burst into tears in desperation over the suffering of beings all around him. One of his tears fell into a lotus, says the pious tale, and from that lotus was born Tara. But the tears came first.

Dear God —
 Could You watch things for a while? I need a nap....

One of the secrets of surviving as a person who prays for others is to create time-outs when you simply will not help others. It may seem cruel and uncaring, but it is necessary unless you want to be a casualty yourself in this difficult world. I call this "fasting from blessing."

Have mercy on yourself. Do pray for others; but when you find your eyes growing red and your sense of humor going away, give it a rest. Just refuse to help for a while.

 Inflation

Inflation is that wonderful feeling that you are God's favorite, or perhaps an avatar. It's very similar to taking too much responsibility — it just feels better. The wind is at your back, your sail is full, and you're scudding across the spiritual sea. It's the sensation that you are God's personal representative on earth, or the hottest thing the Dharma ever incarnated, or the Goddess's pet. It is the sort of feeling that comes when there have been a string of successful treatments.

Humor is the best cure for inflation — a sense or irony and the habit of not taking yourself too seriously. There is another and less kind cure for inflation: it will go away just as soon as you encounter disaster.

The famous Metaphysical teacher Emma Curtis Hopkins told Religious Science founder Ernest Holmes of a convention she held in Chicago, where a student, an Absolutist, began screaming, "I am God!" She said, "There, there, George, it is all right for you to play you are God, but don't be so noisy about it."[139]

 Failure

Ah, failure. You have prayed for someone, and they just up and died. What can you say? If it was someone you love, you grow angry and guilty at the same time. Angry at God or all your allies. Guilty because you didn't try hard enough or do it right; or because you believed in this stuff in the first place.

It's a double blow. It is the feeling that you have lost not only someone you love, but also your faith, all at once.

I will try not to say something platitudinous like "It's God's will." But I do want to tell you the stories of Jim and Abigail.

Jim Summers was a lovely man, funny and skillful and kind. He was a floor director for Jacques Pepin's cooking shows, and Pepin loved his work. He would appear on the set with a whisk around his neck on a string, over a T-shirt that said "Taste the Whip." He was that kind of wit. He was also a musician and a gardener and good company.

When he was diagnosed with AIDS it was sudden and heartbreaking. He had survived being a gay child in a Mormon mountain town, and he had survived most of the AIDS epidemic in San Francisco. But three months after his first positive test he was in the hospital in the Castro district of the city. We went to visit him, sure that this was only an episode and that the new protease inhibitors would save him. Three of us did treatment on him, to ease his discomfort as much as anything.

Instead of making him feel better, we seemed to make him more uncomfortable. We left, feeling bad; and three days later Jim died at three in the morning. It was shattering for me. We had lost a friend and had been no help at all.

Except that . . .

Jim had told all his friends that he wanted to die young. He had seen others waste away from the disease. He had made the standard joke about "leaving a beautiful corpse." After he died, his family attended a memorial service for him in San Francisco, and found out how many people valued their son. Jacques Pepin and his daughter Claudine were there, and they spoke to each member of Jim's family about how important Jim had been to their show and to them personally. A reconciliation that could not happen in life seemed to happen at his death.

Abigail was "just a dog." We loved her extravagantly, as childless couples do with their pets. When she got suddenly sick I rushed her to the veterinarian, who took one look at her and said she must have immediate surgery. I called Nancy, my wife, who came quickly to the veterinary office; then I called my friends who pray and asked them to pray for Abigail's recovery.

The surgery was a near thing. She had a massive internal infection, and it was a masterwork of surgery to get it out without damaging her organs. But two vets did it, and Abigail recovered. It seemed a miracle, of veterinary medicine and prayer both. One of the people praying for Abigail said, "She stayed because she knew how sad you'd be."

Except that . . .

Abigail recovered physically, but her mind wandered. She lost all control over her bladder in the next few months, and couldn't chase kites on the beach or do any of the things she loved. She had Alzheimers, it turned out, and by the time she died she did not even recognize her own house. If she had died in that surgery, it would have been after a good life, and while she was still clear and alive.

Did Jim die quickly because he wanted to and because that was for the best? Did Abigail live on because we forced her to, beyond her own best time to go? I don't know; I really do not know. I think about Jim and Abigail a lot, though, when I pray for others.

Unworthiness and Guilt

And what if you are not worthy to pray? What if you have a deep guilt that tells you that you should not approach the altar of God?

I would not presume to play psychology with you and deny your sense of guilt. It is possible that it's inaccurate — that nothing is wrong with you — and it is possible that you have indeed done something to be guilty about.

Maybe you are uncomfortable with your own personality. You think you are not kind enough, not tolerant enough, not generous enough, too irascible, too impatient, or too lazy. You may have struggled with an addiction for years. You may not like yourself.

Guilt and unworthiness are very painful and make it difficult to think of anything else. For all that, our guilt is irrelevant. When we turn to pray for other people, we are in that moment being worthy. It does not matter why we do it, or what psychological landscape we pray from. In that

157

Lord, I am not worthy that Thou shouldst enter under my roof. Say but the word, and my soul shall be healed.

— Roman Catholic Mass

moment we are being kind, and kindness is a good place to begin.

If you are guilty, you may need to do penance. May I suggest that the most appropriate penance is to lay aside the whip with which you punish yourself? If you are guilty, it's your most treasured possession. But as your penance, put it aside while you pray for others. Prayer for others is about them, not about you.

 Knowing Our Role

My mother spent some time in the theater, and she used to say, "You're padding your part." It meant that I was making my role in something larger than it really was.

All four of these things — over-responsibility, inflation, a sense of failure, and guilt — come from thinking our part in this process is larger than it is. When we pray or treat for another person, we call for help from something much larger than we are, and we ask that something to do its best — *the* best — in the situation. So immediately we have to admit that we aren't sure what is best. Yes, of course, this uncertainty can be a rationalization for failure. But even if our beliefs and our practices are true and appropriate, we find ourselves in a situation where we don't know. We guess, but we are not sure, that it is better for Jim and Abigail to live.

This is why people so frequently add a disclaimer to their prayers. "If it is Thy will," say Christians and Jews.

"Inshallah," say Muslims, "If Allah wills it." "May all beings be happy," say Buddhists. "May it be for the best for all concerned," says each person in their heart, as best they can. It is a way of reminding ourselves that we are the junior partners.

We don't know what is best, and still we need to try to know. Consider the Golden Rule from Jesus, a rule with strong antecedents in Jewish thought. It's a tricky thing to figure out what it means. Does it say that if you like hot chipotle peppers, you should sprinkle them on everyone else's potatoes? When your back itches, you should scratch other people's backs? No, it must mean something a little more subtle — like doing whatever others need. But is that the same thing as doing what they want?

Therefore all things whatsoever ye would that men should do to you, do ye even so to them: for this is the law and the prophets.
— Matthew 7:12 KJV

It doesn't take long to discover that the Golden Rule is actually a meditation question, a *koan* that requires your attention again and again. And as your meditation on it continues, different answers come forth.

One that came for me is that I need to accept the prayers and blessings of others. It's frustrating to be praying for another person, quite sure that I'm praying for their real good, and to feel a resistance pushing back. "It's as if you're talking to a wall," says Religious Science practitioner and minister Margaret Stortz.

And one of the most gratifying things I know is to feel someone gratefully accepting a blessing, taking it into the house and watering it until it grows bright and green. Again in the words of Margaret Stortz: " ... the sense of internal all-rightness that takes place in them, a sense of completion. A sense of something having moved, if you will, whether it's completely manifested or not, something's moved in here. The inner, internal sense that you get, that something is in place."

If it feels so good to a blesser to know that a blessing has been accepted, I think those who would bless need to accept blessings too. That means to receive, not just put out; to be a guest sometimes instead of insisting on being the host.

In order to "do unto others," then, you need to relax, to let go, accept the same blessings you're handing out. And if you refuse to do so, you have to ask yourself, "Why?" What special status do you have to make yourself better than the people you're praying for? Jesus took time off; many of the stories about him say that he was at a party or sitting with friends. Buddha took time off, and sat with his disciples. But *you*, oh no, not you.

So — please take this advice very seriously (as long as we're being very serious about all this). Please accept for yourself as you would want others to accept from you. Let us do that, then, right now: Let us lay aside the prayers through which we have been blessing other people throughout this book, and open ourselves to blessings instead. Let the good wishes of others come towards us. Let those blessings be shaped in wisdom, motivated by good will, and full of power. Let us accept the blessings that are sent to us.

Part of the intention of the "Golden Koan" is to find out what we have put into our blessings. In addition to our good wishes, there are all the flavors of our joy and sadness mingled into the way we pray for others.

In American Sign Language, the sign for "good" is made by raising your open hand to your face, and then lowering it in front of you. The image is of smelling something, and then (having found that it is pleasant) offering it to others. As we accept the sorts of blessing we offer to other people, we may find out if our blessings are palatable and good to receive.

It is like tasting the soup you plan to serve to your guests, to make sure that there is not too much salt or bitterness in it. But a little salt and the bitterness of herbs can make it good. Failure and uncertainty reduce our arrogance and make both us and our prayers better. Sometimes it happens that the sadness has, mysteriously, become the blessing.

ENOUGH WORDS

Rain drips from palm fronds.
All heaven made these drops, that
Wash leaves, water earth.

The royal road to progress in spiritual understanding is to solve *definite* problems by prayer.

Emmet Fox said: "Every time you heal any condition, however small, by prayer, whether you are working for yourself or someone else, you gain an increase in spiritual understanding. One definite healing, whether it be of the body or of anything else, will teach you more about spiritual truth than hours of discussion or reading."[140]

NOTES

1. I hope the endnotes will lead you to more information if you want it. The dissertation is Birrell Walsh, "The Practice of Praying for Others: Eight Examples from Late Twentieth-Century America" (California Institute for Integral Studies, 1999). It is based on interviews with eight people. I wrote up what they did, how they prayed, and then asked them to comment on it.

2. Lawrence LeShan, *The Medium, the Mystic, and the Physicist: Toward a General Theory of the Paranormal* (New York: Ballantine, 1974).

3. James 1:27.

4. Genesis 28.

5. Genesis 32.

6. Ezekiel 2.

7. Acts 9.

8. William James, *The Varieties of Religious Experience* (New York: Modern Library, 1902).

9. 1 Kings 19.

10. Arnold Mindell, Ph.D., *Dreaming While Awake: Techniques for Twenty-Four-Hour Lucid Dreaming* (Charlottesville, Va.: Hampton Roads, 2000).

11. Louis Savary and Patricia H. Berne, *Kything: The Art of Spiritual Presence* (Mahwah, N.J.: Paulist Press, 1980).

12. Ibid.

13. Julie Henderson, *The Lover Within: Opening to Energy in Sexual Practice* (Barrytown, N.Y.: Station Hill, 1986, 1999).

14. Rose Rosetree, *Empowered by Empathy: Twenty-Five Ways to Fly in Spirit* (Sterling, Va.: Women's Intuition Network, 2000).

15. Ibid.

16. The Greek word for "virtue" in this passage is *dunamis*. It is the word that we would use if we were to translate the modern words "power" or "energy" into the Greek of Jesus' time.

17. Both the real and the imitation Therapeutic Touch sessions were videotaped, and a panel of observers was asked if they could distinguish the real TT from the imitation. They were not able to do

so. Nevertheless the real TT produced significantly more benefit. See Janet F. Quinn, "Therapeutic Touch as Energy Exchange: Testing the Theory," *Advances in Nursing Science* 6, no. 2 (1984).

18. Michael Crichton, *Travels* (New York: Ballantine Books, 1988).

19. Dora Kunz, *Spiritual Healing* (Wheaton, Ill.: Quest Books, 1995).

20. Versions of the story are available in Anonymous, "The History of the Usui Healing System," ed. Traditional Japanese Reiki Association (*www.reikilinks.com/home/tjreiki/history.html*: 1998), Bodo J. Baginski and Shalila Sharamon, *Reiki: Universal Life Energy*, trans. Christopher Baker and Judith Harrison (LifeRhythm, 1988), Kasja Krishni Borang, *Thorsons Principles of Reiki* (Thorsons Publications, 1998), Helen J. Haberly, *Reiki: Hawayo Takata's Story* (Olney, Md.: Archedigm Publications, 1990), Paula Horan, *Empowerment through Reiki* (Wilmot City, Wisc.: Lotus Light, 1992), and Diane Stein, *Essential Reiki: A Complete Guide to an Ancient Healing Art* (Freedom, Calif.: Crossing Press, 1995). Sources for much Reiki history and information online in 2002 are *www.threshold.ca/reiki*.

21. Haberly, *Reiki: Hawayo Takata's Story*.

22. I interviewed Dr. Stuckey in 1999. Her quotations come from Walsh, "The Practice of Praying for Others: Eight Examples from Late Twentieth-Century America."

23. Haberly, *Reiki: Hawayo Takata's Story*.

24. Borang, *Thorsons Principles of Reiki*.

25. Janet Quinn, "Therapeutic Touch Frequently Asked Questions" (*www.haelanworks.com/therapeutic_touch_faq.htm*, 2002). For detailed instructions see Dolores Krieger, *Accepting Your Power to Heal: The Personal Practice of Therapeutic Touch* (Santa Fe, N.Mex.: Bear and Company, 1993) and Janet Macrae, *Therapeutic Touch: A Practical Guide* (New York: Alfred A. Knopf, 1987).

26. This quote and many of the studies are assembled online at *www.haelanworks.com/research.htm*.

27. On her website at *www.haelanworks.com/therapeutic_touch_faq.htm#How does TT work*.

28. Crichton, *Travels*.

29. Matthew 18:19–20 KJV.

30. There are several organizations with this name. At this writing (2003) one website for the healing order is *www.orderofstluke.org*.

31. Glenn Clark, *I Will Lift Up Mine Eyes* (Carmel, N.Y.: Guideposts Associates, 1940).

32. Or "Hasidim." My informant about this tradition was a Lubavitcher rabbi. He preferred the spelling "Chassidim," so I use it.

33. Matthew 26:38.

34. I worked with Harry Monohan, and he told me this story some years before his death.

35. George W. Cronyn, *The Path on the Rainbow: An Anthology of Native American Songs and Chants* (North Hollywood, Calif.: Newcastle Publishing Co., 1918, 1997).

36. Sean Kelly and Rosemary Rogers, *Saints Preserve Us!: Everything You Need to Know about Every Saint You'll Ever Need* (New York: Random House, 1993).

37. Vessantara, *Meeting the Buddhas: A Guide to Buddhas, Bodhisattvas, and Tantric Deities* (Glasgow: Windhorse, 1993).

38. Winthrop Sergeant, *The Bhagavad Gita*, ed. Antonio T. de Nicolas, Suny Series in Cultural Perspectives (Albany: State University of New York Press, 1984) 9:23.

39. This story is told in more detail (and lovely words) in Hazel Deane, *Powerful Is the Light*, 60–62.

40. W. Frederic Keeler, *Solving the Problem of Supply*, ed. Alma Morse (Oakland, Calif., Lakeside Temple of Practical Christianity, 1971).

41. The Greek for this makes a pretty good mantra: *Teknon, su pantote met' emou ei kai panta ta ema sa estin*. It comes from the story of the prodigal son, where the father says it to the son who has stayed home and tried to be good. Quite a promise, isn't it?

42. Ernest Holmes, *Your Invisible Power* (Los Angeles: Science of Mind Publications, 1974).

43. Ibid.

44. In *The Nature of Personal Reality*, 12, quoted in Nancy Ashley, *Create Your Own Reality: A Seth Workbook* (Englewood Cliffs, N.J.: Prentice Hall, 1984).

45. Catherine Ponder, *The Dynamic Laws of Prayer* (Marina del Rey, Calif.: DeVorss, 1987).

46. Ernest Holmes, *How to Use the Science of Mind* (New York: Dodd Mead, 1948).

47. Emmet Fox, *Make Your Life Worthwhile* (New York: Harper & Brothers, 1946).

48. Mary Katherine MacDougall, *What Treasure Mapping Can Do for You* (Unity Village, Mo.: Unity School of Christianity, 1986).

49. David Spangler, *Everyday Miracles: The Inner Art of Manifestation* (New York: Bantam, 1996).

50. Walsh, "The Practice of Praying for Others: Eight Examples from Late Twentieth-Century America."

51. Ernest Holmes, *The Science of Mind* (New York: Dodd Mead, 1938).

52. Libellus XI:ii in Waltern Scott, *Hermetica: The Ancient Greek and Latin Writings Which Contain Religious or Philosophic Teachings Ascribed to Hermes Trismegistus* (Boston: Shambhala, 1985, 1993).

53. Emmet Fox, *The Seven Main Aspects of God* (Marina del Rey, Calif.: DeVorss, 1942).

54. Mary Baker Eddy, *Science and Health, with Key to the Scriptures* (Boston: First Church of Christ, Scientist, 1890).

55. Fox, *Make Your Life Worthwhile.*

56. For instance, Marsilio Ficino in his *Commentary on Plato's Symposium.*

57. Robert Owen (pseud. of John Klingbeil), *The Healer* (Salem, Ore.: Grayhaven Books, 1985).

58. *Science and Health,* 460.

59. Larry Dossey, *Be Careful What You Pray For. . . . You Just Might Get It* (San Francisco: HarperSanFrancisco, 1997).

60. In Pseudo-Dionysius, *The Divine Names* IV.17 in Colm Luibheid, translator, *Pseudodionysius the Areopagite: The Complete Works,* ed. John Farina, The Classics of Western Spirituality (New York/Mahwah: Paulist Press, 1987).

61. Stuart Grayson, *Spiritual Healing: A Simple Guide for the Healing of Body, Mind, and Spirit* (New York: Simon & Schuster, 1997).

62. Stephen Olsson, *My House in Havana* (television program) (Public Broadcasting System, 2000).

63. Rose Rosetree, *Aura Reading through All Your Senses* (Sterling, Va.: Women's Intuition Worldwide, 1996).

64. Robert Peel, *Spiritual Healing in a Scientific Age* (San Francisco: Harper & Row, 1987), 141.

65. W. Frederic Keeler, *Christian Victory Instruction,* ed. Alma Morse (Oakland, Calif.: Lakeside Temple of Practical Christianity, 1983).

66. Lee Coit, *Listening: How to Increase Awareness of Your Inner Guide* (Wildomar, Calif.: Las Brisas Publishing, 1985).

67. Ibid.

68. 2 Chronicles 1:10–12.

69. 2 Chronicles 9:1–12.

70. Michael Harner, *Hallucinogens and Shamanism* (New York and London: Oxford, 1973).

71. Michael Harner, *The Way of the Shaman: A Guide to Power and Healing* (New York: Bantam Books, 1982).

72. Robert Oswalt, *Kashaya Texts,* vol. 36, *University of California Publications in Linguistics* (Berkeley and Los Angeles: University of California Press, 1964), quoted in Harner, *The Way of the Shaman: A Guide to Power and Healing.*

73. For the diagnostic role of hand-tremblers among the Navajo, see Åke Hultkrantz, *Shamanic Healing and Ritual Drama: Health and Medicine in Native North American Religious Traditions*, Health/Medicine and the Faith Traditions, ed. James P. Wind and Martin E. Marty (New York: Crossroad, 1992). For more information, see Alexander Hamilton Leighton and Dorothea Cross Leighton, *Gregorio, the Hand-Trembler: A Psychobiological Personality Study of a Navaho Indian*, Reports of the Ramah Project No. 1, Papers of the Peabody Museum of American Archaeology and Ethnology, Harvard University, vol. 40, no. 1 (Cambridge, Mass.: The Museum, 1949).

74. Alvaro Estrada, *Maria Sabina: Her Life and Chants*, ed. Jerome Rothenberg, trans. Henry Munn, *New Wilderness Poetics* (Santa Barbara: Ross-Erikson, 1981).

75. These are Nancy Grant's words. She is a singer and a musician, trained at the New England Conservatory of Music.

76. Sandra Ingerman, *Soul Retrieval: Mending the Fragmented Self* (San Francisco: HarperSanFrancisco, 1991).

77. This is said to be from G. V. Ksendofotov, quoted in Henri F. Ellenberger, *The Discovery of Dynamic Psychiatry* (New York: Basic Books, 1970), 7, and quoted in turn in ibid. But it is probably G. V. Ksenofontov, who wrote *Legendy i rasskasy o shamanakh u yakutov, buryat i tungusov* (Moscow, 1930), which had a German translation by A. Friedrich and Georg Buddruss called *Schmanengeschichten aus Sibirien* (Munich and Planegg, 1955), both of which are in the bibliography of Mircea Eliade, *Shamanism: Archaic Techniques of Ecstasy*, Bollingen Series (New York: Princeton, 1964). Thought you would want to know.

78. Ingerman, *Soul Retrieval*.

79. Piero Ferrucci, *Psychosynthesis* (New York: Crown, 1979).

80. As the Japanese Shinto sun-goddess Amaterasu saw her own glory in a mirror outside her cave, in the Shinto tale.

81. See Ambrose A. Worrall and Olga N. Worrall, *The Gift of Healing: A Personal Story of Spiritual Therapy* (Columbus Ohio: Ariel Press, 1965, 1985) and Edwina Cerutti, *Mystic with the Healing Hands: The Life Story of Olga Worrall* (San Francisco: Harper and Row, 1975).

82. Worrall and Worrall, *The Gift of Healing: A Personal Story of Spiritual Therapy*.

83. Cerutti, *Mystic with the Healing Hands*.

84. Eliade, *Shamanism*.

85. Lama Thubten Yeshe et al., *The Bliss of Inner Fire: Heart Practice of the Six Yogas of Naropa* (Boston: Wisdom Publications, 1998).

86. Broderick Barker, "If Christ Has Done All, What Could I Do?," *San Diego News Notes*, 1999.

87. See Sylvester P. Juergens, S.M., *The New Marian Missal for Daily Mass* (New York: Regina Press, 1959).

88. *www.scj.org/scj_homp/dehoniana/2001/3-2001/3-2001-06-eng.html*.

89. Mary Costello, "To Offer or Not to Offer (It Up)? It's a Lenten Thing," *The Catholic Advocate on the Web*, 2/13/2002.

90. Juergens, *The New Marian Missal for Daily Mass*.

91. The story of Arlette was quoted online at *www.scj.org/scj_homp/dehoniana/2001/3-2001/3-2001-06-eng.html*.

92. *www.calmspirit.com/dedi.htm*.

93. From "A Basic Dharma Practice" at *www.enlightenment.com/practice/webster/basic.html*.

94. This story too is from *www.scj.org/scj_homp/dehoniana/2001/3-2001/3-2001-06-eng.html*.

95. Max Freedom Long, *Mana, or Vital Force* (Cape Girardeau, Mo.: The Huna Fellowship, 1981).

96. Ibid.

97. Dr. Henderson's first work on energy is Julie Henderson, *The Lover Within: Opening to Energy in Sexual Practice*. Her more recent work on energy and space is published in German and English: Julie Henderson, *Embodying Well-Being* (Napa, Calif.: Zapchen, 1999). The story of her work at the retreat is told with her permission.

98. The Sanskrit is: "Om dharmādharmahavidīpte ātmāgnau manasā srucā Suşumnā vartmana nityamakŗavşttirjuhomyaham." From Agehananda Bharati, *The Tantric Tradition* (New York: Anchor Books, 1965).

99. Birrell Walsh, "Diotima: The Lost Teacher of Socrates," *The Quest* 4, no. 2 (1991).

100. Shams-ud-din Muhammad Hafiz, *The Gift: Poems by Hafiz, the Great Sufi Master*, trans. Daniel Landinsky (New York: Penguin Compass, 1999).

101. "Divine Names" 713b–c in Luibheid, *Pseudodionysius the Areopagite: The Complete Works*.

102. A story very similar to this (so help me) true account is told in R. A. MacAvoy, *Twisting the Rope* (New York: E-Rights, E-Reads, Ltd., 1986, 2000). I have to wonder on what experience MacAvoy based her novel.

103. Miranda Shaw, *Passionate Enlightenment: Women in Tantric Buddhism* (Princeton: Princeton, 1994).

104. Xenophanes said of Pythagoras: "Once they say that he was passing by when a puppy was being whipped, and he took pity and said:

'Stop, do not beat it; for it is the soul of a friend that I recognized when I heard it giving tongue.'"

105. Martin Palmer, *The Jesus Sutras: Rediscovering the Lost Scrolls of Taoist Christianity* (New York: Ballantine Wellspring, 2001).

106. Acharya Buddharakkhita, *Metta: The Philosophy and Practice of Universal Love* (Kandy, Sri Lanka: 1995).

107. Anguttara Nikaya, Ekadasa Nipata 16, in Thich Nhat Hanh, *Teachings on Love* (Berkeley, Calif.: Parallax Press, 1997).

108. Buddharakkhita, *Metta: The Philosophy and Practice of Universal Love*, at www.accesstoinsight.org/lib/bps/wheels/wheel365.html. This practice of using metta to calm elephants continues today in Burma and Sri Lanka, according to Mirko Fryba, *The Art of Happiness: Teachings of Buddhist Psychology*, trans. Michael H. Kohn (Boston: Shambhala, 1989). Fryba adds, "For a first exercise in *metta*, however, one should not choose a large animal."

109. K. Sri Dhammananda, *Daily Buddhist Devotions* (Kuala Lumpur: Buddhist Missionary Society, 1991).

110. Sutta Nipata, volume 1, cited in Nhat Hanh, *Teachings on Love*.

111. Bhadantacariya Buddhaghosa, *Visuddhimagga: The Path of Purification*, trans. Bhikku Nyanamoli, 2 vols. (Berkeley and London: Shambhala, 1976).

112. Fryba, *The Art of Happiness: Teachings of Buddhist Psychology*.

113. Matthew 22:37–39.

114. Mary Jo Meadow, *Gentling the Heart: Buddhist Loving-Kindness Practice for Christians* (New York: Crossroad, 1994).

115. Lama Thubten Yeshe, *Introduction to Tantra: A Vision of Totality* (Boston: Wisdom, 1987), 114.

116. John 17:21 KJV.

117. John 15:5 KJV.

118. John 15:6 KJV.

119. This mantra will "work" better if one has an initiation from an accomplished master.

120. Shaw, *Passionate Enlightenment: Women in Tantric Buddhism*.

121. Walsh, "The Practice of Praying for Others: Eight Examples from Late Twentieth-Century America."

122. Acts 17:28.

123. Marsilio Ficino, *Meditations on the Soul: Selected Letters of Marsilio Ficino* (Rochester, Vt.: Inner Traditions International, 1996).

124. Marion Weinstein, *Magic for Peace: A Non-Sectarian Guide to Working Positive Magic for Peace and Safety* (New York: Earth Magic Productions, 1991).

125. Joel Goldsmith, *The Contemplative Life: A New Text for Personal Growth and Extended Awareness* (Secaucus, N.J.: University Books, 1963).

126. Elaine Aron and Arthur Aron, *The Maharishi Effect* (Walpole, N.H.: Stillpoint, 1986).

127. Anonymous, *A Book of Contemplation the Which Is Called the Cloud of Unknowing, in Which a Soul Is Oned with God* (London: John M. Watkins, 1922).

128. W. Frederic Keeler, *The Practice of Christian Healing: An ABC Course,* ed. Alma W. Morse (Oakland, Calif.: Lakeside Temple of Practical Christianity, 1971).

129. W. Frederic Keeler, *Lessons in Applied Metaphysics,* vol. 2, ed. Alma Morse (Oakland, Calif.: Lakeside Temple of Practical Christianity, 1987).

130. Keeler, *Christian Victory Instruction.*

131. Keeler, *The Practice of Christian Healing: An ABC Course.*

132. Anonymous, *The Cloistered Poor Clare Nuns* (The Poor Clare Federation of Mary Immaculate in the United States of America, 1993).

133. Clark, *I Will Lift Up Mine Eyes.*

134. Imam Rashid Patch is a member of Imam Hyde's community, and often gives the call to prayer. He explained the reference: "When Muhammad was asked to call damnation down on unbelievers who were stoning members of the young Muslim community, he refused. 'I was not sent to curse,' he said."

135. Aryeh Kaplan, *Meditation and Kabbalah* (York Beach, Maine: S. Weiser, 1982).

136. Ibid.

137. Robert Young, *Young's Literal Translation of the Holy Bible,* rev. ed. (Grand Rapids: Baker Book House, 1956).

138. Martin Buber, *Tales of the Hasidim: Early Masters* (New York: Schocken Books, 1947).

139. Paraphrased from Fenwicke Holmes, *Ernest Holmes: His Life and Times* (New York: Dodd Mead, 1970).

140. Fox, *Make Your Life Worthwhile.*

BIBLIOGRAPHY

Anonymous. *A Book of Contemplation the Which Is Called the Cloud of Unknowing, in Which a Soul Is Oned with God.* London: John M. Watkins, 1922.

———. *The Cloistered Poor Clare Nuns:* The Poor Clare Federation of Mary Immaculate in the United States of America, 1993.

———. "The History of the Usui Healing System." Edited by Traditional Japanese Reiki Association. *www.reikilinks.com/home/tjreiki/history.html*, 1998.

Aron, Elaine, and Arthur Aron. *The Maharishi Effect.* Walpole, N.H.: Stillpoint, 1986.

Ashley, Nancy. *Create Your Own Reality: A Seth Workbook.* Englewood Cliffs, N.J.: Prentice Hall, 1984.

Astin, John A., Ph.D., Elaine Harkness, and Edzard Ernst, M.D., Ph.D. "The Efficacy of 'Distant Healing': A Systematic Review of Randomized Trials." *Annals of Internal Medicine* 132, no. 6 (June 2000): 903–10.

Baginski, Bodo J., and Shalila Sharamon. *Reiki: Universal Life Energy.* Translated by Christopher Baker and Judith Harrison: LifeRhythm, 1988.

Barker, Broderick. "If Christ Has Done All, What Could I Do?" *San Diego News Notes,* 1999.

Benor, Daniel J. *Healing Research: Holistic Energy Medicine and Spirituality,* vol. 1, *Research in Healing.* Munich: Helix Verlag, 1993.

Bharati, Agehananda. *The Tantric Tradition.* New York: Anchor Books, 1965.

Borang, Kasja Krishni. *Thorsons Principles of Reiki:* Thorsons Publications, 1998.

Buber, Martin. *Tales of the Hasidim: Early Masters.* New York: Schocken Books, 1947.

Buddhaghosa, Bhadantacariya. *Visuddhimagga: The Path of Purification.* Translated by Bhikku Nyanamoli. 2 vols. Berkeley and London: Shambhala, 1976.

Buddharakkhita, Acharya. *Metta: The Philosophy and Practice of Universal Love.* Kandy, Sri Lanka, 1995.

Byrd, Randolph C. "Positive Therapeutic Effects of Intercessory Prayer in a Coronary Care Unit Population." *Southern Medical Journal* 81, no. 7 (1988): 826–29.

Cerutti, Edwina. *Mystic with the Healing Hands: The Life Story of Olga Worrall.* San Francisco: Harper and Row, 1975.

Clark, Glenn. *I Will Lift Up Mine Eyes.* Carmel, N.Y.: Guideposts Associates, 1940.

Coit, Lee. *Listening: How to Increase Awareness of Your Inner Guide.* Wildomar, Calif.: Las Brisas Publishing, 1985.

Costello, Mary. "To Offer or Not to Offer (It Up)? It's a Lenten Thing." *The Catholic Advocate on the Web,* 2/13/2002.

Crichton, Michael. *Travels.* New York: Ballantine Books, 1988.

Cronyn, George W. *The Path on the Rainbow: An Anthology of Native American Songs and Chants.* North Hollywood, Calif.: Newcastle Publishing Co., 1918, 1997.

Dhammananda, K. Sri. *Daily Buddhist Devotions.* Kuala Lumpur: Buddhist Missionary Society, 1991.

Dossey, Larry. *Be Careful What You Pray For . . . You Just Might Get It.* San Francisco: HarperSanFrancisco, 1997.

———. *Healing Words: The Power of Prayer and the Practice of Medicine.* San Francisco: HarperSanFrancisco, 1993.

Eddy, Mary Baker. *Science and Health, with Key to the Scriptures.* Boston: First Church of Christ, Scientist, 1890.

Eliade, Mircea. *Shamanism: Archaic Techniques of Ecstacy,* Bollingen Series. New York: Princeton, 1964.

Estrada, Alvaro. *Maria Sabina: Her Life and Chants.* Translated by Henry Munn. Edited by Jerome Rothenberg. *New Wilderness Poetics.* Santa Barbara: Ross-Erikson, 1981.

Ferrucci, Piero. *Psychosynthesis.* New York: Crown, 1979.

Ficino, Marsilio. *Meditations on the Soul: Selected Letters of Marsilio Ficino.* Rochester, Vt.: Inner Traditions International, 1996.

Fox, Emmet. *Make Your Life Worthwhile.* New York: Harper & Brothers, 1946.

———. *The Seven Main Aspects of God.* Marina del Rey, Calif.: DeVorss, 1942.

Fryba, Mirko. *The Art of Happiness: Teachings of Buddhist Psychology.* Translated by Michael H. Kohn. Boston: Shambhala, 1989.

Goldsmith, Joel. *The Contemplative Life: A New Text for Personal Growth and Extended Awareness.* Secaucus, N.J.: University Books, 1963.

Grayson, Stuart. *Spiritual Healing: A Simple Guide for the Healing of Body, Mind, and Spirit.* New York: Simon & Schuster, 1997.

Haberly, Helen J. *Reiki: Hawayo Takata's Story.* Olney, Md.: Archedigm Publications, 1990.

Hafiz, Shams-ud-din Muhammad. *The Gift: Poems by Hafiz, the Great Sufi Master.* Translated by Daniel Landinsky. New York: Penguin Compass, 1999.

Hagelin, John, David Orme-Johnson, Maxwell Rainforth, Kenneth Cavanaugh, and Charles N. Alexander. "Results of the National Demonstration Project to Reduce Violent Crime and Improve Governmental Effectiveness in Washington, D.C., June 7 to July 30, 1993." 1–55. Fairfield, Iowa: Institute of Science, Technology and Public Policy, 1994.

Harner, Michael. *Hallucinogens and Shamanism.* New York and London: Oxford, 1973.

———. *The Way of the Shaman: A Guide to Power and Healing.* New York: Bantam Books, 1982.

Harris, William S., Ph.D., Manohar Gowda, M.D., Jerry W. Kolb, M.Div., Christopher P. Strychacz, Ph.D., James L. Vacek, M.D., Philip G. Jones, M.S., Alan Forker, M.D., James H. O'Keefe, M.D., and Ben D. McCallister, M.D. "A Randomized, Controlled Trial of the Effects of Remote, Intercessory Prayer on Outcomes in Patients Admitted to the Coronary Care Unit." *Archives of Internal Medicine* 159 (1999): 2273–78.

Henderson, Julie. *Embodying Well-Being.* Napa, Calif.: Zapchen, 1999.

———. *The Lover Within: Opening to Energy in Sexual Practice.* Barrytown, N.Y.: Station Hill, 1986, 1999.

Holmes, Ernest. *How to Use the Science of Mind.* New York: Dodd Mead, 1948.

———. *The Science of Mind.* New York: Dodd Mead, 1938.

———. *Your Invisible Power.* Los Angeles: Science of Mind Publications, 1974.

Holmes, Fenwicke. *Ernest Holmes: His Life and Times.* New York: Dodd Mead, 1970.

Horan, Paula. *Empowerment through Reiki.* Wilmot City, Wisc.: Lotus Light, 1992.

Hultkrantz, Åke. *Shamanic Healing and Ritual Drama: Health and Medicine in Native North American Religious Traditions.* Health/Medicine and the Faith Traditions, edited by James P. Wind and Martin E. Marty. New York: Crossroad, 1992.

Ingerman, Sandra. *Soul Retrieval: Mending the Fragmented Self.* San Francisco: HarperSanFrancisco, 1991.

James, William. *The Varieties of Religious Experience.* New York: Modern Library, 1902.

Juergens, Sylvester P., S.M. *The New Marian Missal for Daily Mass.* New York: Regina Press, 1959.

Kaplan, Aryeh. *Meditation and Kabbalah.* York Beach, Maine: S. Weiser, 1982.

Keeler, W. Frederic. *Christian Victory Instruction.* Edited by Alma Morse. Oakland, Calif.: Lakeside Temple of Practical Christianity, 1983.

———. *Lessons in Applied Metaphysics,* vol. 2. Edited by Alma Morse. Oakland, Calif.: Lakeside Temple of Practical Christianity, 1987.

———. *The Practice of Christian Healing: An ABC Course.* Edited by Alma W. Morse. Oakland, Calif.: Lakeside Temple of Practical Christianity, 1971.

———. *Solving the Problem of Supply.* Edited by Alma Morse. Oakland, Calif.: Lakeside Temple of Practical Christianity, 1971.

Kelly, Sean, and Rosemary Rogers. *Saints Preserve Us!: Everything You Need to Know about Every Saint You'll Ever Need.* New York: Random House, 1993.

Kelsey, Morton. *Healing and Christianity in Ancient Thought and Modern Times.* New York: Harper & Row, 1973.

Klingbeil, Bruce, and John Klingbeil. *The Spindrift Papers,* vol. 1, 1975–1993, *Exploring Prayer and Healing through the Experimental Test.* Salem, Ore.: Spindrift, 1993.

Klingbeil, Deborah. *Spirit Tracking.* Racine, Wisc.: Grayhaven CSN, 2001.

Kraft, Dean. *Portrait of a Psychic Healer.* New York: Putnam, 1981.

Krieger, Dolores. *Accepting Your Power to Heal: The Personal Practice of Therapeutic Touch.* Santa Fe, N.Mex.: Bear and Company, 1993.

Kunz, Dora. *Spiritual Healing.* Wheaton, Ill.: Quest Books, 1995.

Leighton, Alexander Hamilton, and Dorothea Cross Leighton. *Gregorio, the Hand-Trembler: A Psychobiological Personality Study of a Navaho Indian,* Reports of the Ramah Project No. 1, Papers of the Peabody Museum of American Archaeology and Ethnology, Harvard University, vol. 40, no. 1. Cambridge, Mass.: The Museum, 1949.

LeShan, Lawrence. *The Medium, the Mystic, and the Physicist: Toward a General Theory of the Paranormal.* New York: Ballantine, 1974.

Loehr, Franklin. *The Power of Prayer on Plants.* Garden City, N.Y.: Doubleday, 1959.

Long, Max Freedom. *Mana, or Vital Force.* Cape Girardeau, Mo.: The Huna Fellowship, 1981.

Luibheid, Colm, translator. *Pseudodionysius the Areopagite: The Complete Works.* Edited by John Farina. The Classics of Western Spirituality. New York/Mahwah: Paulist Press, 1987.

MacAvoy, R. A. *Twisting the Rope.* New York: E-Rights, E-Reads, Ltd., 1986, 2000.

MacDougall, Mary Katherine. *What Treasure Mapping Can Do for You.* Unity Village, Mo.: Unity School of Christianity, 1986.

Macrae, Janet. *Therapeutic Touch: A Practical Guide.* New York: Alfred A. Knopf, 1987.

Meadow, Mary Jo. *Gentling the Heart: Buddhist Loving-Kindness Practice for Christians.* New York: Crossroad, 1994.

Mindell, Arnold, Ph.D. *Dreaming While Awake: Techniques for Twenty-Four-Hour Lucid Dreaming.* Charlottesville, Va.: Hampton Roads, 2000.

Nhat Hanh, Thich. *Teachings on Love.* Berkeley, Calif.: Parallax Press, 1997.

Olsson, Stephen. *My House in Havana* (television program). Public Broadcasting System, 2000.

Oswalt, Robert. *Kashaya Texts.* Vol. 36, *University of California Publications in Linguistics.* Berkeley and Los Angeles: University of California Press, 1964.

Owen, Robert (pseud. of John Klingbeil). *The Healer.* Salem, Ore.: Grayhaven Books, 1985.

Palmer, Martin. *The Jesus Sutras: Rediscovering the Lost Scrolls of Taoist Christianity.* New York: Ballantine Wellspring, 2001.

Peel, Robert. *Spiritual Healing in a Scientific Age.* San Francisco: Harper & Row, 1987.

Ponder, Catherine. *The Dynamic Laws of Prayer.* Marina del Rey, Calif.: DeVorss, 1987.

Quinn, Janet. "Therapeutic Touch Frequently Asked Questions." *www.haelanworks.com/therapeutic_touch_faq.htm,* 2002.

Quinn, Janet F. "Therapeutic Touch as Energy Exchange: Testing the Theory." *Advances in Nursing Science* 6, no. 2 (1984): 42–49.

Rosetree, Rose. *Aura Reading through All Your Senses.* Sterling, Va.: Women's Intuition Worldwide, 1996.

———. *Empowered by Empathy: Twenty-Five Ways to Fly in Spirit.* Sterling Va.: Women's Intuition Network, 2000.

Savary, Louis and Patricia H. Berne. *Kything: The Art of Spiritual Presence.* Mahwah, N.J.: Paulist Press, 1980.

Scott, Waltern. *Hermetica: The Ancient Greek and Latin Writings Which Contain Religious or Philosophic Teachings Ascribed to Hermes Trismegistus.* Boston: Shambhala, 1985, 1993.

Sergeant, Winthrop. *The Bhagavad Gita.* Edited by Antonio T. de Nicolas. Suny Series in Cultural Perspectives. Albany: State University of New York Press, 1984.

Shaw, Miranda. *Passionate Enlightenment: Women in Tantric Buddhism.* Princeton: Princeton, 1994.

Solfvin, Gerald F. "Psi Expectancy Effects in Psychic Healing Studies with Malarial Mice." *European Journal of Parapsychology* 4, no. 2 (1982): 160–97.

Spangler, David. *Everyday Miracles: The Inner Art of Manifestation.* New York: Bantam, 1996.

Stein, Diane. *Essential Reiki: A Complete Guide to an Ancient Healing Art.* Freedom, Calif.: Crossing Press, 1995.

Vessantara. *Meeting the Buddhas: A Guide to Buddhas, Bodhisattvas, and Tantric Deities.* Glasgow: Windhorse, 1993.

Walsh, Birrell. "Diotima: The Lost Teacher of Socrates." *The Quest* 4, no. 2 (1991): 50–55.

———. "The Practice of Praying for Others: Eight Examples from Late Twentieth-Century America." Dissertation, California Institute for Integral Studies, 1999.

Weinstein, Marion. *Magic for Peace: A Non-Sectarian Guide to Working Positive Magic for Peace and Safety.* New York: Earth Magic Productions, 1991.

Worrall, Ambrose A., and Olga N. Worrall. *The Gift of Healing: A Personal Story of Spiritual Therapy.* Columbus, Ohio: Ariel Press, 1965, 1985.

Yeshe, Lama Thubten. *Introduction to Tantra: A Vision of Totality.* Boston: Wisdom, 1987.

Yeshe, Lama Thubten, Blo-bzaçn-grags-pa Tsoçn-kha-pa, Robina Courtin, and Ailsa Cameron. *The Bliss of Inner Fire: Heart Practice of the Six Yogas of Naropa.* Boston: Wisdom Publications, 1998.

Young, Robert. *Young's Literal Translation of the Holy Bible.* Rev. ed. Grand Rapids: Baker Book House, 1956.

STUDYING PRAYER

The effect of prayer is being studied, and that study is not new. In the Torah[1] is the story of the competition between Moses and Aaron and the magicians of Pharaoh, and in the lives of the prophets are repeated challenges to prove their claims with miracles. The forty-one healings performed by Jesus could be seen as practical demonstration of the effectiveness of blessing in many forms, from words to touch to the power of the recipient's faith. Augustine thought the age of miracles was over in the early fifth century, but by his later writings he had changed his mind and ordered that miraculous healings in his diocese be tabulated.[2]

A number of modern studies have found that prayer and blessing work.

In 1988 Randolph Byrd published research he had done at the University of California Medical Center. Several hundred cardiac patients were enrolled in a "double-blind" study in which neither patients nor caregivers knew which patients were in the treatment and which in the control group. Patients who received intercessory prayer did significantly better.[3] That is, they were five times less likely to require antibiotics, three times less likely to develop pulmonary edema. None of the prayed-for patients required endotracheal intubation and ventilator support. They were also less likely to die.[4]

A similar study with nearly a thousand patients was published in the *Archives of Internal Medicine*. It came to the cautious conclusion that "Remote, intercessory prayer was associated with lower CCU course scores. This result suggests that prayer may be an effective adjunct to standard medical care."[5]

In 2000 the *Annals of Internal Medicine* published a very careful review of studies of the effectiveness of "distant healing." The criteria for inclusion were extremely stringent: research was excluded if it had "lack of randomization, no adequate placebo condition, use of nonhuman experimental subjects or nonclinical populations," and had not been published in peer-reviewed journals. Consider what would happen to medical drug research if, say, studies of nonhuman experimental subjects were excluded. But even with these very difficult criteria, 57 percent of the studies in the report showed significant positive results. Therapeutic Touch did particularly well.[6]

Puzzling Research

After you have been involved in praying for others for a while, you make strange discoveries. You find that different styles of prayer — even your favorite — are not easily correlated with success or failure. You notice that some people bring ease and coherence to an environment without consciously intending to do so. You notice that clearly miraculous healings may happen without anyone praying for them. If you are confused, it may be a comfort to know that professional researchers are just as puzzled.

Nothing here will contradict the good news that prayer often seems to work. But some of the research that's been done about prayer and blessing can leave us baffled. There are studies that seem to show that (1) There are at least two different kinds of prayer results — and no way to be sure which you'll get; (2) blessings can happen without intention on the part of the blesser, as a by-product of meditation; and, maybe the most mysterious of all, (3) sometimes prayer does not even need an agent — a pray-er — to heal.

Prayer can have two different kinds of results. One could be called "goal-referenced" and the other kind of result could be called "identity-referenced."

Christian Science practitioner Bruce Klingbeil found that his church was not willing to test scientifically the results of Christian Science treatment, and as a result the modern world was regarding it as superstition. Parents who relied on Christian Science treatment for their children were being prosecuted and sent to jail if the children died, although no one was sent to jail if a child died under medical care.

Klingbeil was convinced that the effectiveness of Christian Science healing could be proven if he could find the right sort of tests, and that training for healers could be based on those tests. He needed to operationalize, to make testable in modern terms, a traditional Christian Science distinction between spiritual healing and faith healing. That distinction and some of the Klingbeil family's work was discussed in the chapter about goal and pattern-based prayer.

The Christian Science tradition believes that both faith healing and spiritual healing can act non-locally on others. Faith healing, as they understand it, works towards a human goal (which may be good or not), while spiritual healing "impels a system to those norms of state or action that are best for the system," or "identity-referenced results."[7]

Armed with the concept that different forces were at work, the Klingbeils were able to design experiments to look for corresponding different sorts of results.

They did find that there were two different kinds of outcomes. While goal-referenced results moved the recipients in one direction (toward the goal), identity-referenced results might move the recipients in a variety of ways.

The goal-referenced prayer results tend to be "more of something" or "less of something." For instance, in his famous and influential early study of the effectiveness of prayer,[8] Rev. Franklin Loehr prayed for grass seedlings as they sprouted. He measured the effectiveness of prayer by how much *taller* the prayed-for grass seedlings grew than the control seedlings did. In other studies of healing, the goal is lessening something. Energy healer Dean Kraft took part in experiments in which he calmed the activity of a mouse.[9]

The Klingbeils did experiments in seed germination just like Franklin Loehr's. But they would soak two different groups of seeds in opposite ways. One group would be over-soaked, until the seeds were waterlogged. The other group would be under-soaked and too dry. Then the two groups would be prayed for at the same time. When the results were IR (identity-referenced), the under-soaked seeds would take up water when compared with un-prayed-for controls. The over-soaked seeds would emit water compared with the controls. Both sets of seeds would approach the norm of "just moist enough."[10] But if you had a statistical test based on the assumption that everything changes in the same direction, you might find very little change in the average. You can find IR results statistically, but to design the test properly you have to have some sense of what is best for the organism.

Because you may not know what the best is, IR results can be completely unexpected. Deborah Klingbeil talked about praying for a developmentally disabled adult who lived with his mother. He ended up in the hospital and then in a group home. The mother was devastated. But her son was making real friends and having some independence for the first time. It was not what Deborah Klingbeil had expected, however. Just because you aspire to perceive the spiritual pattern doesn't mean that you can predict what will happen in the physical universe when identity-referenced prayer results occur.

Perhaps nothing will happen. If the organism is at its norm, no change at all will occur. This is very different from goal-referenced (GR) prayer results. If you pray that just-about-normal sprouting seedlings get bigger and get GR results, they may grow to be over-large and stringy. If you get IR results, they won't change much at all. They are fine just as they are. This is a good thing, of course; but it can make you think the method is not working. The Klingbeils did find that the norm itself might gradually evolve over time when the organism was prayed for.

The Klingbeils developed ingenious tests to distinguish between IR and GR results. One test involved yeast, whose growth you can measure by watching how much CO_2 it is producing. Young, fresh yeast tends to concentrate its growth in the early period of its life, so the graph of its growth curve has a bulge near the left (beginning) side. As yeast gets middle-aged, the growth-curve's bulge moves to the middle of the graph.

If someone prays for middle-aged yeast, the growth curve can show whether the prayer results are GR or IR. If the prayer-result is goal-referenced, the bulge stays in the middle but gets bigger. There is more growth, yes, but without a change in pattern. But if the prayer result is identity-referenced, the bulge moves toward the left, and the curve resembles that of young yeast.

One of their findings is that most people have a mixture of prayer results. But even with relatively pure GR or IR results, the Klingbeils made a startling discovery: It is not (yet) possible to predict which sort of results you will get from what sort of prayer you pray. Deborah Klingbeil explains: "I can pray a very directed prayer and get an IR result. I can pray a very open prayer and get a GR result. Two Christian Science practitioners can pray the same way and get different results. Two Catholics can both pray the rosary; one will get an IR result and one will get a GR. I think it is misleading to say if you pray in a non-directed way, for example, that you will get an IR result, because the studies have surprisingly shown this is not true."

She described a study in which people were asked to visualize people's temperature coming down. The recipients of the prayer did not have a fever, in fact, but were lying for the sake of the study. Some of those who visualized made someone's temperature come down — they hurt them — and others who also visualized the temperature coming down did not, they got an IR result. So some goal referenced style prayer produced a GR result and others an IR result. "Why, we don't know. More study is needed."

These results are credible just because they're different from what the Klingbeils hoped to show. They wanted to establish that Christian Science treatment worked, and to distinguish between identity-referenced and goal-referenced prayer. They did show that there are two different kinds of prayer results — but that those results do not necessarily correlate with the kind of prayer being used.

Blessing Without Intention

Beginning with one study in 1974, followers of the Maharishi Mahesh Yogi seem to have established that Transcendental Meditation has a remarkable result. The practice of TM by a small percentage of a population would improve the quality of social life for the whole local population, even for those who were not practicing the meditation and who did not know that the meditation was going on.

In an enthusiastic book, *The Maharishi Effect*,[11] by Elaine and Arthur Aron (both social scientists, and both TM meditators), there is not just a suggestive study, or even one well-constructed experiment, but a whole series of tests. The authors know statistical methodology very well, as that is what they teach professionally. They manage to explain the methodology for people who don't understand it, so that the reader can appreciate the increasing sophistication of the questions that were brought to the hypothesis and (one by one) answered.

The first set of tests simply established that there was a correlation. That is, when the proportion of meditators in a society reached one percent, the crime rate fell. Follow-up tests confirmed that the effect would be found in other cities. Researchers used progressively more sophisticated statistical tools to confirm the correlation, first cross-lagged panel analysis and, later, time-series analysis. They found that the associations were genuine, and further that TM practice was preceding the improvements in "social coherence." Finally they attempted to show that there was a causal relation, not just a correlation.

They were able to establish causal relations by doing "true experiments." If a local TM population was the cause, they should be able to create the improved social conditions by creating a local threshold-level TM group. Using the organizational resources of the TM movement, they moved people in and out of areas. When the meditators were there, social indicators improved. When the meditators left, the indicators returned to their former levels.

The experiment was tried at various scales. One experiment moved small groups of meditators into various neighborhoods in Atlanta, Georgia. The indicators responded. Another experiment gathered meditators in centers of conflict like Israel and Nicaragua. Again the indicators tracked with their presence. In one summer, enough TM meditators were brought to Rhode Island to cross the threshold. Because most social indicators are kept by state, extremely detailed results could be obtained. By comparing them with the same season in other years, and with the exact same time in another small state (Delaware), researchers could be relatively sure that TM was the cause of the changes.

Of what changes, you might ask. Decreases in suicide, homicide, death, cirrhosis, traffic fatality, robbery, aggravated assault, breaking and entering, unemployment, cigarette sales rates, and even improvements in pollution levels and the weather.

I have a 1994 preliminary report from an experiment to reduce crime and improve governmental efficiency in Washington, D.C. Results indicated that there was a drop of up to 18 percent in police "radio run calls" during the test period — and a simultaneous rise in support for the president during the test period.[12]

It seems that most meditators do not sit and think, "I am going to increase social coherence." In fact the effective part of their meditation is free of any thought — in TM jargon, it is called "the experience of pure consciousness."

We have to admit that most of the meditators have probably heard of the social effect of meditation. In some cases they have even assembled to test it, as they did in Rhode Island, so the amount of intention involved was probably greater than zero, but less than focused purpose.

Nevertheless, groups of people were able to bring about documented blessings for their environment without focused purpose. They were blessing others without that being their primary intention, and their results were repeatable.

Healerless Healing

In 1982 Gerald Solfvin published in Europe an article with an unexciting name, "Psi expectancy effects in psychic healing studies with malarial mice."[13] A summary is available in Daniel Benor's book on healing.[14] Despite the name, the results were startling.

Solfvin inoculated mice with a form of malaria. He told his handlers — students in a veterinary school — that a psychic healer would work on some of their mice. Which mice were to be treated was concealed carefully. Half of the mice had been designated by a random process as the "to-be-healed" group. Two different people conducted the randomizing process, in three steps. Solfvin did not know which mice were in which group, nor did the handlers. In fact, the mice in the to-be-healed group did significantly better. So far, this experiment is like many other well-designed double-blind experiments.

The strange part of the study is — there was no healer. Solfvin had lied to his handlers about the existence of a healer. That is, there was a healing effect on the mice who had been designated, but no one to cause the effect. The handlers did not know which mice were designated, nor did Solfvin until after the results were in, and there was no healer at work — and still the designated mice did "significantly" better (that is, the probability that the results were by chance was less than 1 in 20). Solfvin commented that: "We have therefore produced a paranormal healing effect, or something that re-sembles a healing effect, in a well controlled laboratory study which cannot be attributed to a specific psychic healer or heal-ing treatment. It must therefore be attributable to something else and that something else may be operating in other psychic healing situations as well."[15]

I think the implications far out-reach Solfvin's conservative comment. Double-blind experiments are based on the idea that if no one knows who is receiving the treatment until after the results are in, there can be no experimenter effect. Solfvin's experiment seems to show an experimenter effect in just those circumstances. It reaches beyond parapsychology to rock the foundations of experimental science, because *it undercuts the idea of double-blind experiments.*

It also has implications for anyone who believes that it is focused intention that heals. There was no focus possible because no one knew which mice were to be healed, and therefore no one who was blessing those mice directly. Yet they did significantly better than their untreated fellows. Researcher Lawrence LeShan told the following similar story on himself:

"However all results must be evaluated cautiously. The most dramatic single result I had occurred when a man I know asked me to do a distance healing for an extremely painful condition requiring immediate and intensive surgery. I promised to do the healing that night, and the next morning when he awoke a 'miraculous cure' had occurred.

"The medical specialist was astounded, and offered to send me pre- and post-healing X-rays and to sponsor publication in a scientific journal. It would have been the psychic healing case of the century except for one small detail. In the press of overwork, I had forgotten to do the healing! If I had only remembered, it would have been a famous demonstration of what can be accomplished by this method."[16]

Three Steps into Humility

These three studies are presented here to encourage a healthy uncertainty about the agents, methods, and intentions by which prayer works. In each of the three studies something surprising happened.

Two generations of the Klingbeil family found that there are two different kinds of prayer result — but they have not discovered how to produce them reliably. This means that neither method of prayer is guaranteed to be better, at least in terms of the goal-referenced/identity-referenced distinction.

The Transcendental Meditation researchers found that their form of meditation blessed people as a by-product. The meditators did not need to intend to make things better or to have any intention at all. The only thing they had to do was gather in sufficient numbers and meditate, and social indicators would begin to change for the better. Here there was a method and there were agents — but the intention was minimal.

Solfvin showed that very specific healing effects — improvement for a "to be treated" group as opposed to a control group — could take place without any obvious agent or method or intention. No one was consciously doing any healing or even knew which mice were in the treatment group. And still the "to be treated" mice did significantly better.

Fullness of knowledge always means some understanding of the depths of our ignorance; and then is always conducive to humility and reverence.   — Robert Millikan[17]

All three forms of "treatment" produced benefits for those who received them. It seems clear that even though blessing is an ancient practice and serious researchers have shown that it works, we really don't know much about it. We do not yet know all it can do, in part because we do not yet know how it works. What an opportunity!

Already we know that blessing often works. This book has hoped to show some of the many ways one can cook in a prayer kitchen, and that it is perfectly legitimate (and an old custom) to borrow recipes from each other.

Each recipe for prayer means we can be of service to more people. One day you pray for a distant friend by unifying them with the Good they need. Another day you feel inexplicably called to rest your hands on an aching back and let energy come through you. You have more ingredients in your storeroom, so you can serve more needs.

Please, don't forget to rest now and then. Keep your sense of humor. And may you prepare and taste many good blessings!

There is an open group on Yahoo for people who practice prayer for others:

http://groups.yahoo.com/group/prayerforothers

You can join it by sending an email (no subject or body is needed; you are only communicating with Yahoo's robot) to: *prayerforothers-subscribe@yahoogroups.com.*

Notes to Studying Prayer

1. Exodus 7.
2. Morton Kelsey, *Healing and Christianity in Ancient Thought and Modern Times* (New York: Harper & Row, 1973).
3. Randolph C. Byrd, "Positive Therapeutic Effects of Intercessory Prayer in a Coronary Care Unit Population," *Southern Medical Journal* 81, no. 7 (1988).
4. Larry Dossey, *Healing Words: The Power of Prayer and the Practice of Medicine* (San Francisco: HarperSanFrancisco, 1993).
5. William S. Harris, Ph.D. et al., "A Randomized, Controlled Trial of the Effects of Remote, Intercessory Prayer on Outcomes in Patients Admitted to the Coronary Care Unit," *Archives of Internal Medicine* 159 (1999).
6. John A. Astin, Ph.D., Elaine Harkness, and Edzard Ernst, M.D., Ph.D., "The Efficacy of 'Distant Healing': A Systematic Review of Randomized Trials," *Annals of Internal Medicine* 132, no. 6 (June 2000).
7. Robert Owen (pseud. of John Klingbeil), *The Healer* (Salem, Ore.: Grayhaven Books, 1985).
8. Franklin Loehr, *The Power of Prayer on Plants* (Garden City, N.Y.: Doubleday, 1959).
9. Dean Kraft, *Portrait of a Psychic Healer* (New York: Putnam, 1981).
10. Bruce Klingbeil and John Klingbeil, *The Spindrift Papers*, vol. 1, 1975–1993, *Exploring Prayer and Healing through the Experimental Test* (Salem, Ore.: Spindrift, 1993).
11. Elaine Aron and Arthur Aron, *The Maharishi Effect* (Walpole, N.H.: Stillpoint, 1986), 115.
12. John Hagelin et al., "Results of the National Demonstration Project to Reduce Violent Crime and Improve Governmental Effectiveness in Washington, D.C., June 7 to July 30, 1993" (Fairfield, Iowa: Institute of Science, Technology and Public Policy, 1994).

13. Gerald F. Solfvin, "Psi Expectancy Effects in Psychic Healing Studies with Malarial Mice," *European Journal of Parapsychology* 4, no. 2 (1982).

14. Daniel J. Benor, *Healing Research: Holistic Energy Medicine and Spirituality*, vol. 1, *Research in Healing* (Munich: Helix Verlag, 1993).

15. Ibid.

16. LeShan, *The Medium, the Mystic, and the Physicist: Toward a General Theory of the Paranormal*.

17. *www.leadershipnow.com/humilityquotes.html.*

ABOUT THE AUTHOR

Birrell Walsh is moderator of an online prayer group for Buddhists and others, and is the former owner of the interfaith Religious Humor list. During the 1990s he examined styles of intercessory prayer as practiced in North America. His research led to his Ph.D. in comparative religion at the Institute for Integral Studies.

He is on the staff of public television station KQED and has written for *MicroTimes*, *Marketplace* on Public Radio International, *Byte* magazine, *Gnosis* magazine, *The Quest*, *Whole Earth Review*, and *Unity* magazine. He lives with his wife, Nancy Grant, in San Francisco.

Readers are invited to join the Praying for Others online group by visiting *http://groups.yahoo.com/group/prayingforothers* or by e-mail at *prayingforothers-subscribe@yahoogroups.com*.